LINDA SIMON was born in 1946 in New York City. She received her B.A. from Queens College, in New York, and her M.A. from New York University. She is currently teaching at Fordham University in New York, and is working on a new book about Alice B. Toklas. GERTRUDE STEIN: A COMPOSITE PORTRAIT is her first book.

GERTRUDE STEIN

A COMPOSITE PORTRAIT

Edited by
LINDA SIMON

DISCUS BOOKS/PUBLISHED BY AVON

AVON BOOKS
A division of
The Hearst Corporation
959 Eighth Avenue
New York, New York 10019

First Discus Printing, November, 1974.

DISCUS TRADEMARK REG. U.S. PAT. OFF. AND
FOREIGN COUNTRIES, REGISTERED TRADEMARK—
MARCA REGISTRADA, HECHO EN CHICAGO, U.S.A.

Printed in the U.S.A.

The editor wishes to thank Donald Gallup of the Bienecke Library of Yale University and Rita Myers of the Museum of Modern Art for their kind efforts.

CONTENTS

GERTRUDE STEIN:
A Composite Portrait

INTRODUCTION

Identity always worries me
and memory and eternity.

Everybody's Autobiography

She could be domineering, stubborn, disdainful; ingenuous, sensitive, enthusiastic. Some remember her cold, scornful eyes, some her hearty, playful laughter, her exuberance and wit. If we set memory beside memory, portrait beside portrait, there emerges the multiplicity of moods and energies that was Gertrude Stein.

The popular image of Gertrude Stein—second only to Einstein, she told us, as the foremost creative mind of the twentieth century—was clearly her own invention. When she sailed for France in 1903 she left behind the tormented, depressed "outlaw" who could not live in America. Few who shared her life in Paris

11

knew of the fears of her youth. "I never had an unhappy anything," she told them in *Everybody's Autobiography*. "What is the use of having an unhappy anything."

But the early years were difficult. She grew up, after all, in what she called "early Victorian" America, and was expected to fulfill first the role of dutiful daughter and later of model wife.

Her father, like a German Jewish Clarence Day, was authoritarian and given to bursts of irrational anger. "Naturally my father was not satisfied with anything," she recalled. Her mother, a characteristic Victorian wife, always acquiesced to her husband's wishes and was rather ineffectual with the children.

Gertrude Stein realized early that she was "the most cut off" from the rest of her family. She could not share with them her thoughts and true feelings. Even her brother Leo, with whom she would romp through the hills of California talking of books and people, later remembered that they never spoke of their inner life. "She knew nothing about mine and I knew nothing about hers."

Her imagination was stirred by the books she read voraciously. Shakespeare, Trollope, Defoe all took her far from the mundane middle-class world of Oakland, California, far from the fears she felt living in a world where she was solitary and not understood. "When she was a little one sometimes she wanted not to be existing," she wrote of herself. At times, she thought of the unutterable solution to her desolate feelings: "I wish I had died when I was a little baby and had not any feeling, I would not then have to be always suffering. . . ."[1]

The feelings that frightened her "between babyhood and fourteen" became crystallized in mid-adolescence. These were "dark and dreadful days" beginning the long, slow process of disillusionment and alienation which was not to culminate until her twenty-ninth year.

She was nearing the age when she would be expected to do "nothing in the wide world except the tasks of the peacock, the spreading of his tail before an admiring audience." She knew what was expected of her: to marry, to be "willing to take everything and be satisfied to live in Belmont in a large house with a view and plenty of flowers and neighbors who were cousins and some friends who did not say anything."[2]

The only recourse was college, and for a while Gertrude Stein was on her way toward fulfilling the feminist ideal of the liberated woman. At Radcliffe it did not matter that she was not "a vigorous specimen of self-satisfied American girlhood." She was bright and imaginative and able to succeed despite her unfeminine appearance. "She always wore black, and her somewhat ample figure was never corseted. She was, in fact, frequently untidy in appearance and her garments were not always neat," recalled a classmate from Harvard.[3]

But fashion was not on the mind of Gertrude Stein. At Radcliffe she was finally able to allow her individuality to emerge, to try to understand her identity as a woman and to grapple with the passions and sexual longings which had caused her feelings of profound confusion and guilt. College was "freedom physical and mental freedom," she wrote later. It was the only way she could escape from the prescribed fate so willingly accepted by most of her contemporaries. She was trying to find a personal liberation from the society that oppressed her, and believed then that education was the right road. From Radcliffe, she went on to medical school at Johns Hopkins. Her decision, though not unheard of, was bold for the age in which she lived, and she was reprimanded by a former classmate for being one of those "deluded and pitiable . . . young women who are aspiring after what is beyond them in our own day."[4]

But Gertrude Stein was not deluded as were many young feminists. She did not desire liberation into a man's world, for she saw that men were hardly more liberated than women. They were "job-chasers," turned from free men into employees, doomed to failure by industrialism which "makes 'em stop thinking, stop feeling makes 'em all feel alike."

Mass production, thought Stein, had put America squarely and certainly in the twentieth century. But at the same time she worried about Americans becoming increasingly "employee-minded" and losing their pioneering spirit. "How I hate that word job," she wrote.[5] And yet she, too, seemed to have a job in her future. As a doctor, she would be among the elite of American career women. Through her undergraduate years, and through her first years at Johns Hopkins, she managed to suppress her rejection of the American dream of success, of femininity, of personal fulfillment. She tried to conform, listening to the inner voice that warned her she would have to submit sooner or later. "Be still, it is inevitable," she tried to make herself believe.[6]

But it became apparent that what was inevitable for others was impossible for Gertrude Stein. A spiritual exile, she was often driven into the madness and solitude that she termed "the Red Deeps." Then, in her final year at medical school, she was forced to confront her singularity once more. This time she found herself inexorably set apart from her society.

Unable to hide her feelings any longer, she succumbed to a strong attraction for May Bookstaver, a fellow student at the University. But when Stein revealed for the first time the emotions that had for years tormented her, May cruelly mocked her for her innocence and naïveté and found companionship with a more sophisticated woman.

Stein's sufferings were so intense that she failed several courses in her medical studies and could not graduate with her class. That summer she joined her brother Leo in Tangiers, Granada, and Paris. But she returned once more to America. The following year she spent the spring in Italy and the summer in London. She found London dismal and depressing; even the offerings of the reading room at the British Museum were not sufficient to distract her. She sailed back to New York for the winter and shared an apartment on Riverside Drive. She began to write in earnest. In the spring she sailed to Paris—and stayed.

Although later she was flippant about leaving medical school, claiming to have been exceedingly bored, it was not boredom that sent her back and forth from America to Europe, but a search for refuge, for a world which would accept a "strange being" like herself.

Paris, she found, "was the place to be." It was in Paris that the legend of Gertrude Stein was created and nurtured. In Paris she was free to be "a genius." The recollections which make up this volume are of that Gertrude Stein: the cheerful eccentric, the literary anarchist, the woman who defiantly declared:

I shall not speak for anybody. I shall do my duty. I shall establish that mile. I shall choose wonder.[7]

Notes

[1] In the character of Martha Hersland in *The Making of Americans* Stein offers a portrait of her own childhood. Something Else Press reissued (1966) Stein's first version; an abridged version is published by Harcourt, Brace (1966) and includes a preface by her friend and translator, Bernard Faÿ.

[2] "If You Had Three Husbands" *Geography and Plays,* Something Else Press, 1968.

[3] A typescript of Arthur Lachman's memoir of Gertrude Stein, "Gertrude Stein As I Knew Her," is deposited in the Stein collection of the Bienecke Rare Book Library at Yale University.

[4] Letter from Margaret Sterling Snyder to Gertrude Stein on April 29, 1896 appears in *Flowers of Friendship,* edited by Donald Gallup, Knopf, 1953.

[5] cf. *Brewsie and Willie,* Random House, 1946.

[6] The college theme quoted here was written on December 20, 1894. Other brief essays, written in the winter of 1894 and the spring of 1895 for an English course at Radcliffe are printed in Rosalind S. Miller's *Gertrude Stein: Form & Intelligibility,* Exposition Press, 1949.

[7] "Pink Melon Joy" *Geography and Plays, op. cit.*

FERNANDE OLIVIER

After a provincial upbringing and an unhappy marriage at seventeen, Fernande Olivier escaped into the lively world of the artists who populated Montmartre at the beginning of the twentieth century. As a child she had been taken to the Louvre and shown the paintings her parents admired. Like many lower-class Parisians, they preferred artists who closely imitated nature; they themselves were makers of artificial flowers. Her own appreciation of modern art began in the Luxembourg Museum, where she found Renoir, Degas, Monet, her "beloved Manet," and Cézanne. "My reaction was immediate and powerful," she recalled, far different from her early docile feelings about art. The Impressionists not only painted a more vibrant world but lived in one. Among the artists she met in Montmartre was Dufy, who risked the derision of the masters at the conservative Ecole des Beaux-Arts to carry on his colorful explorations.

Mlle. Olivier had been living at 13 rue Ravignan for only a short time before "a rather curious person" moved in. Pablo Picasso, having just come back to Paris from Spain in 1903, joined the group of struggling young artists and poets in the shabby building later to be nicknamed the "Bateau-Lavoir." Mlle. Olivier describes herself then as "young, rather timid, enthusiastic and extremely proud." She was also tall and attractive, lithe and elegant, and soon became Picasso's mistress, accompanying him often to Gertrude Stein's studio.

Although Gertrude Stein recalled that the young woman's interests were seemingly limited to hats, perfumes, and furs, and so relegated her to Alice Toklas' care, Mlle. Olivier defends herself:

> There is a tendency in France, particularly amongst intellectuals, to regard women as incapable of serious thought. I sensed this, and it paralyzed me. So I contented myself with listening. I believed in the profundity of the ideas I heard exchanged. I listened, passionately attentive, but I never dared utter an opinion of my own.

If her reticence earned her a somewhat dubious reputation of being merely an attractive fixture, her listening enabled her to observe, and later record, the spirited life of Montmartre and the Latin Quarter.

She watched through Gertrude Stein's sittings for her portrait, entertaining her by reading the fables of La Fontaine. The studio she shared with Picasso was "a picture animated by the wild colour and confusion of the huge canvases he was working on. . . .

> There was a mattress on four legs in one corner. A little iron stove, covered in rust with a yellow earthenware bowl on it, served for washing; a towel and a minute stub of soap lay on a whitewood table beside it. In another corner a pathetic little black-painted trunk made a pretty uncomfortable seat. A cane chair, easels, canvases of every size and tubes of paint were scattered all over the floor with brushes, oil containers and a bowl for etching fluid. There were no curtains. In the drawer of the table was a pet white mouse which Picasso tenderly cared for and showed to everybody.

Amid the clutter, Miss Stein sat patiently until, one day, Picasso blanked out the face, declaring he could no longer see her.

Fernande Olivier watched, too, as Picasso worked through his "blue" period, his "rose" period, his harlequin period. She saw his painting become more geometrical, influenced by archaic Spanish sculpture and the African masks he had just discovered. But, while she was in sympathy with Picasso's art, her relationship with the man was less than stable. The causes of their arguments ranged from accusations about hoarding the comic strips (often given to them by Gertrude Stein's brother Leo) to flares of jealousy. Finally, in 1915, after sharing twelve years of hardship (for two months Fernande couldn't leave the house because she had no shoes), they parted. Picasso then moved to Montparnasse, leaving Fernande Olivier and his Montmartre life forever behind.

In the selection that follows, Mlle. Olivier looks back to those "most precious years" and remembers Gertrude Stein.

🌿 *Fernande Olivier / from* Picasso
and His Friends

I remember how surprised Picasso was one day when
two Americans, brother and sister, visited him. What
an odd couple they were! He looked like a professor,
bald and wearing gold-rimmed spectacles. He had a
long beard with reddish streaks in it and clever eyes.
His large, stiff body fell into curious attitudes, his
gestures were concise and neat. He was a typical American German Jew.

She was fat, short and massive, with a broad, beautiful head, noble, over-accentuated, regular features, and
intelligent eyes, which reflected her clear-sightedness
and wit. Her mind was lucid and organized, and her
voice and her appearance were masculine. Picasso had
met them both at Sagot's, and attracted by the woman's
physical personality he had offered to do her portrait,
before he really knew her.

Both of them were dressed in brown corduroy and
sandals *à la* Raymond Duncan, who was a friend of
theirs. Too intelligent to bother about whether people
found them ridiculous, too sure of themselves to care
what people thought of them, in fact, they were rich, and
he wanted to be a painter. She was a doctor, who wrote
and had been congratulated on her writing by Wells;
a fact which afforded her no little pride.

They understood modern painting—its value as art
and the influence it might have. They were not only
passionate admirers of the *avant-garde* painters and

their works; their feelings about them were intelligent and they had real flair for the subject.

They were immediately *au courant* with what was going on and bought paintings worth eight hundred francs on their very first visit. It was beyond our wildest dreams.

They invited Picasso to dinner, and his friends to their Saturday evening gatherings. Picasso became one of their regular dinner guests, with Matisse, whom he met there.

The Steins lived on rue Fleurus, in a lodge with a studio at the back of a huge house. Their collection of pictures was already superb. They had Gauguins and Cézannes: amongst others, that beautiful portrait of the painter's wife, wearing a blue dress and sitting in a garnet-coloured arm-chair; and many Cézanne water-colours; women bathing against a background of country-landscape. There was a little Manet, not an important one, but wonderfully sensitive; an El Greco; Renoirs—amongst them, *La Baigneuse de dos,* which is so amazingly luminous; some beautiful Matisse works; a Vallotton, as precise and cold as usual, and paintings by Manguin and Puy. There were dozens more, and now they were joined by some of Picasso's.

A pretty mixed bunch used to turn up on those Saturdays. As small-scale patrons of those extraordinary days the Steins did a great deal to make modern artists popular.

A brother of the Steins, who came to live in Paris with his wife, fell passionately in love with painting too, though he had less understanding of it. He enthusiastically built up a collection of works by Picasso and Matisse.

ALICE B. TOKLAS

The biography of Alice B. Toklas is a short piece that Gertrude Stein cryptically titled "Ada." The running narrative chronicles Miss Toklas' life—her close relationship with her mother, her mother's death, the years of keeping house for her father and caring for her brother, the escape to Paris and her meeting with "some one" who caused her to become "happier than anybody else who was living then."

Alice Babette Toklas was born in San Francisco in a home built by her grandfather at 922 O'Farrell Street. Her mother, a petite woman with memorable violet eyes, "was a very serious person who had no particularly serious interests," Alice recalled. She had a special way with flowers, often producing delicate and unusual arrangements—a talent her daughter seems to have inherited. Alice's father, whom a friend once described as "a minister without portfolio" (a minister of state, that is), was reserved, quiet and aloof.

Between the ages of nine and ten, Alice accompanied her parents to Europe, visiting relatives and by chance witnessing Victor Hugo's funeral procession. The following summer she sojourned to Alaska—ten years before the gold rush—where she was indelibly impressed by the lush gardens and wildflowers.

In San Francisco and later in Seattle, where her family had moved, she was educated in private schools

—for a while she was taught by Emma Marwedel, a student of Froebel—and took piano lessons each Saturday morning. To the young Alice, the lessons were uninspiring, if not dull; but an interest in music—instilled by her grandmother, herself a pianist—gradually developed. At the University of Seattle, Alice majored in music; studied with Otto Bendix, a pupil of Franz Liszt; performed admirably in her teacher's recitals; and received a Bachelor of Music degree.

Her mother's illness brought the family back to San Francisco for consultations with physicians, and her death, when Alice was twenty, altered Alice's plans for a musical career. Instead, she found herself the "responsible grand-daughter" in a house filled with opinionated male relatives. As a distraction against domestic boredom, Alice kept her dream of becoming a concert pianist. More than a tenuous vision, her dream soon became a passion and for several years, she admitted, "everything was music." But when the oppressive atmosphere of her grandfather's house required more immediate relief, Alice would escape to Monterey or Pacific Grove, where she would saddle her horse (kept stabled in Monterey) and "ride madly" along the Seventeen-Mile Drive, then a rustic, untamed path; or along the coast to the point at Tres Pinos. She would collect the family's old clothes, sell them to the local junkman and use the proceeds for an elegant luncheon at the Del Monte Hotel. Or she would spend a week or two at Sherman's Rose, an inn whose Spanish proprietress was said to have been General Sherman's mistress, and whose guests included artists and writers.

Away from her family, Alice exchanged the somber, grey garb she usually wore for exotic brocades, Spanish shawls, shimmering Chinese silks. Released from what one friend described as the "stultifying pall" at home, where the stale odor of cigar smoke lingered in the air long after the nightly discussions of local politics, Alice emerged as vibrant and vivacious. Black-haired, attractively plump, she dressed as Carmen for an annual Mardi Gras of the Mark Hopkins Art Institute (a major event of the social season) and won the attention of a tableful of jovial artists who entertained her for the evening.

Though she was witty and well-read and, she admitted, "violently" political,* she never ventured an opinion at her own dinner table. But when she accompanied her piano teacher and his wife to cafes, or attended dinners at the literary Bohemian Club, she was hardly the reticent young woman who darted past her neighbors on O'Farrell Street with downcast eyes.

But a few frivolous moments were not sufficient to dispel immediate frustrations. "She did not like any of the living she was doing then," Stein noted in "Ada." She had by then discarded her musical ambitions, realizing, at 26, that her talent was "fifth rate." Her grandfather died; the household diminished; her brother, whom she had raised and guided devotedly, was now nearly a man. And though San Francisco was still exciting for her, though California would always be "God's country" to her, she began to plan a final escape: to Paris.

In 1906, the earthquake which tumbled the city changed her life. Michael and Sarah Stein, Gertrude's brother and sister-in-law, had rushed home from Paris to inspect damages to their apartment. Leaving most of their growing collection of art in their home on the rue Madame, they carried with them three Matisse paintings —the first to be seen in America—which they showed to their friend Harriet Levy and her next-door neighbor, Alice Toklas. With enticing descriptions of Parisian life, Sarah Stein persuaded the two young women to

*At that time, she was pro-Chinese, anti-Japanese, and like her friends and neighbors on O'Farrell Street, a "good democrat." Later, she became a life-long pacifist.

make a trip abroad. Alice was then 29, and she never returned home.

Francis Rose recalled that Miss Toklas admitted having been engaged twice before she met Gertrude Stein, once to a sailor who died, once to a music professor she disliked. Gertrude Stein alludes to previous relations that Alice had with several women she met at school. But evidently these rejected loves were unequal to Gertrude Stein. It was shortly after their first meeting that Alice moved into the rue de Fleurus studio and assumed her role as Gertrude Stein's secretary, arranger, protector, defender, companion, cook, and gardener. Her duties ranged from sitting with the wives of geniuses to tending a vegetable garden; from pronouncing the definitive version of a story to providing for Gertrude Stein the stability and comfort she needed to conduct her verbal experiments and carry out her art. She made it possible for Gertrude Stein to share her life with someone who was "always loving," and to accept her own sexuality, which had for so long troubled and tormented her. "We were so wifely," Miss Stein mused, and punctuated her works with love songs to the "wife whom I love with all my life . . ."

Alice Toklas has been variously described as a dark gypsy; a forbidding, swarthy-faced shrew with a furry mustache; a shadowy figure often mistaken for the maid. Her wit—sharp, biting, and sometimes cynical—frightened off the less stalwart visitors to Gertrude Stein's salon. It was common knowledge that lack of approval by Miss Toklas was tantamount to a terminated friendship with Miss Stein. But alone, or in the company of intimate friends, Miss Toklas became the deferential "Pussy" and Miss Stein "Lovey" as they lived daily in obvious harmony.

After Gertrude Stein's death in 1946, Miss Toklas became obsessed with the problem of how to see her friend again, sure that such a genius would achieve immortality. After consulting with friends and some priests, she converted to Catholicism, content to await her own immortality and the final reunion. Her last years were passed in an apartment on the rue de la Convention where, bedridden and arthritic, she lived on an income from a fund generously administered by several close friends. She died, at the age of ninety, in 1967 and shares Stein's simple tombstone, designed by Francis Rose, in the Père Lachaise cemetery in Paris.

What is remembered, in the following selection, is the beginning of "a new full life" for Alice B. Toklas.

🌷 *Alice B. Toklas / from* What Is
Remembered

The Michael Steins were living then and for some years after in the rue Madame, in a building built and occupied by a Protestant church. Their enormous living room had been the assembly and Sunday school room. It was lighted on one side by large windows which gave on a garden. On the walls were many pictures.

In the room were Mr. and Mrs. Stein and Gertrude Stein. It was Gertrude Stein who held my complete attention, as she did for all the many years I knew her until her death, and all these empty ones since then. She was a golden brown presence, burned by the Tuscan sun and with a golden glint in her warm brown hair. She was dressed in a warm brown corduroy suit. She wore a large round coral brooch and when she talked, very little, or laughed, a good deal, I thought her voice came from this brooch. It was unlike anyone else's voice—deep, full, velvety like a great contralto's, like two voices. She was large and heavy with delicate small hands and a beautifully modeled and unique head. It was often compared to a Roman emperor's, but later Donald Sutherland said that her eyes made her a primitive Greek.

We were given tea and left shortly afterwards. Gertrude Stein asked me to come to the rue de Fleurus the next afternoon, when she would take me for a walk.

My head was turning with the day's events. After an exquisite dinner I found a book but soon fell asleep. The next morning I unpacked. Harriet thought she would like to lunch in one of the open-air restaurants in the Bois de Boulogne. In which event it would be wise to send word by petit bleu to Gertrude Stein and make my excuses in case I was late. I was by half an hour.

When I got to the rue de Fleurus and knocked on the very large studio door in the court, it was Gertrude Stein who opened it. She was very different from the day before. She had my petit bleu in her hand. She had not her smiling countenance of the day before. She was now a vengeful goddess and I was afraid. I did not know what had happened or what was going to happen.

Nor is it possible for me to tell about it now. After she had paced for some time about the long Florentine table made longer by being flanked on either side by two smaller ones, she stood in front of me and said, Now you understand. It is over. It is not too late to go for a walk. You can look at the pictures while I change my clothes.

The studio walls were covered from *cimaise* to ceiling with pictures. The furniture and objects fascinated me. The big Tuscan table with the three heavy clawed legs is in the dining room, as well as the double-decked Henry IV buffet with its three carved eagles on the top. It was only after wiping these and other pieces of furniture that I fully appreciated their beauty, their details, their proportions. In the room here at the rue Christine there are only a few objects remaining that were then at the rue de Fleurus, seventeenth-century terra-cotta figures of women and several other pieces of Italian pottery.

By the time I had noticed the objects and pieces of furniture, Gertrude Stein had returned to the studio, more like she had been the day before. A smile had broken through the gloom and she laughed again from her brooch. She asked about Harriet, her health, spirits, and wit, speaking of her familiarly as Harriet. Then Gertrude Stein and I took our first walk. In the nearby Luxembourg Gardens she called my attention. Alice, she said, look at the autumn herbaceous border. But I did not propose to reciprocate the familiarity.

The Luxembourg was filled with children around the artificial lake floating their boats; others were rolling hoops with bells as I had in the Parc Monceau when I was a child. The nurses were still wearing their long capes and starched white caps with broad streamers. Through the gardens into the Petit Luxembourg and down the boulevard Saint-Michel Gertrude Stein led me, asking me what books I had read on the steamer and were the Flaubert letters translated into English. She did not like to read or speak anything but English, although she knew German and French.

There were students wearing the colored ribbons indicating which school they belonged to at the Sorbonne. Gertrude Stein said there was a good pastry shop where the cakes and ices were the best on the Left Bank, should we not have something there. Which we did, a praline ice, just like San Francisco. While we were having an ice and some cake at a table on the sidewalk, Gertrude Stein said Harriet and I should dine with her and her brother Saturday evening and meet the painters who would come in the evening.

Opposite on the boulevard Saint-Michel was a line of fiacres, and I took one back to the Magellan. Harriet wanted to know how I had enjoyed the walk. I told her only of the walk and nothing of what had occurred before. She remarked, Just as I thought, and was satisfied.

The next morning, on going over to the Right Bank to draw on my letter of credit at my bank in the Place Vendôme and collect any mail that might be there, I found a most compromising letter from the commo-

dore.* There was no question of my answering it. I
carried it in my handbag into the Tuileries Gardens
where I sat down near the artificial lake and tore the
letter into shreds, hoping when I dropped them into
the lake that no one was seeing me do so. I then walked
up the Champs Elysees to the hotel. Well, that episode
was closed.

I took to walking mornings and afternoons in all
directions and found Paris more and more enchanting.
I had not gone to the Louvre, nor would I until the
following week. I must first become familiar with what
was to be my home town.

Saturday I knocked at the studio door. It was not
Gertrude Stein who opened it but her brother Leo,
not that I would have recognized him by his resemblance to Gertrude Stein. They did not look at all alike.
Gertrude Stein looked like her father's family. The two
brothers looked like each other. Like Gertrude Stein,
Leo was golden, he had a golden beard. Edith Sitwell
told me that when her father had been asked if she
resembled him he had answered, Yes, but she has not
got this, grasping his beard. Like Gertrude Stein, Leo
was clothed in warm brown. They both wore sandals
made in Florence from a model Raymond Duncan had
designed from those he had seen on a Greek vase in the
British museum. Leo had a beautiful springing step and
carried his tall body with incomparable grace. He at this
time was amiable. But later, when he and Gertrude
Stein disagreed about Picasso's pictures and her writing,
he became unreasonable and unbearable.

In the studio with the two Steins there was a small,
very dark and extremely lively young man, Alfred
Maurer, an American painter known to his intimates as
Alfy. He was gay and witty, and enjoyed shocking his

---

*EDITOR'S NOTE: The commodore was "a distinguished
old man" who spent a great deal of time with Miss Toklas on
the voyage from New York to France.

friends. When he was a guest of the Steins at Fiesole, one evening as he was hanging over the terrace looking down at the Arno Valley he sighed, There should be ten thousand houris there. But ten thousand are a great many, Gertrude Stein said. Not for me, said Alfy.

Hélène, the servant, knocked vigorously on the door and announced dinner. Gertrude Stein led us from the studio, locking the door with an American Yale key. The pavillon door close by was open. The first door to the right in the narrow hallway was the dining room. It was small and made smaller by the book shelves on one of its walls. The two double doors facing each other were lined with Picasso water colors and drawings.

As we were sitting down at table there was a loud knocking at the pavillon door. Hélène came to announce, Monsieur Picasso and Madame Fernande, who in an instant came in, much flustered, both of them talking at the same time. Picasso, very dark with black hair, a lock hanging over one of his marvelous all-seeing brilliant black eyes, was explaining in his raucous Spanish voice, You know how as a Spaniard I would want to be on time, how I always am. Fernande, with her characteristic gesture of one arm extended above her head with a Napoleonic forefinger pointing in the air, asked Gertrude Stein to excuse them. The new suit she was wearing, made for the next day's vernissage of the Salon d'Automne, had not been delivered on time and there was of course nothing to do but wait. Fernande was a large heavy woman with the sensational natural coloring of a *maquillage,* her dark eyes were narrow slits. She was an oriental odalisque. The attention she was attracting pleased her and she sat down satisfied.

The dinner was simple but well cooked. Hélène did not know how or like to cook complicated dishes, nor those that took a long time to prepare. She would not consider preparing those delicious French crêpes. But her roasting was perfection. A leg of mutton invariably was a rare treat. She would put it in the oven, go out on an errand in the neighborhood, and would return at the right moment to baste it.

Conversation at table was lively. While we were still at dessert, Hélène came to say that there were guests in the studio. Gertrude Stein left the dining room hurriedly. We followed soon after to find her sitting in a high leather Tuscan Renaissance armchair, her feet resting on several saddle bags piled on one another.

AMBROISE VOLLARD

Ambroise Vollard, supposedly studying law in Paris, preferred to indulge himself in strolling along the quais and browsing in the small shops near the Seine, looking for inexpensive drawings and engravings. He had been, since the age of four, an indefatigable collector, graduating from the pebbles in his parents' garden to the work of unknown artists. But he did not venture into the profession of art dealer until he was in desperate need of money, no longer able to sustain himself on dry crackers and not able to afford even bread. He struck a bargain with a wine merchant he knew, and soon found his way to the homes of wealthy collectors. With his profits, he left the Montmartre garret in which he had been living and opened a shop on the rue Lafitte, which was, in the early 1900s, the *rue des tableaux*.

Since this notary's son had no formal training and was not himself an artist, his response to art was purely instinctive. Among the piles of canvases in his eclectic collection were the first Cézannes exhibited in Paris—canvases he had purchased from the art supplier Père Tanguy in Montmartre—along with Bonnards, Matisses, Picassos.

As Gertrude Stein described him, Vollard, when cheerful, "was a huge dark man glooming. When he was really cheerless he put his huge frame against the glass door that led to the street, his arms above his head, his hands on each upper corner of the portal and gloomed darkly into the street. Nobody thought then of trying to come in."

Leo Stein at first thought the gallery seemed almost like a junk shop, with a "queer picture" displayed from time to time in the window. He would have passed it by, but on the advice of his friend Bernard Berenson, the art critic, he went in and, as he put it, "was launched" as a collector.

The shop, and especially the cellar where Vollard had his kitchen and dining room, was a meeting place for young artists and writers. Vollard gave parties, luncheons, dinners, and charmed his guests with witty remarks delivered in his gentle lisping accent. The menu usually included chicken curry, the national dish of the island of La Réunion, where Vollard was born. In return for his moral and financial support, many artists —Cézanne, Renoir, Rouault, Bonnard, Picasso— honored him with a portrait. Picasso reported, in fact, that the artists painted Vollard with a keen sense of competition, each wanting to outdo the other.

Vollard became, also, a publisher of art books of uniformly high quality and proportionate price. "My idea was to obtain engravings from artists who were not engravers by profession, and the result was a great artistic success." He persuaded Marc Chagall to illustrate Gogol, Picasso to provide etchings and woodcuts for Balzac's *Chef d'Oeuvre Inconnu,* Emile Bernard to illustrate *Les Fleurs du Mal*. With the help of Dufy, Degas, Rouault, Ambroise Vollard *éditeur,* was established.

Vollard was, along with Daniel-Henry Kahnweiler, a visionary in modern art, exhibiting work that no one else would have, catapulting to success the unknown artists who would become the masters of the twentieth century.

🌸 *Ambroise Vollard / from* Recollections
of a Picture Dealer

One morning, on the rue de Gramont, I received a
visit from a very distinguished-looking woman.

"I am the Marquise de S——" she told me. "I would
like very much to see the Matisses and Picassos that
belong to Mr. Stein. They tell me you know him."

"You need no introduction, madame," I answered.
"There are no more welcoming people in the world
than the Steins, the two brothers and their sister Mlle.
Gertrude. Their door is open to all, on Saturdays from
9:00 P.M. on."

"So I've been told, but today is Monday; I have to
take the train to Rome by the day after tomorrow at
the latest. Imagine what it's like at tea at the Ritz—
everyone spoke of the Stein collection and I—I looked
quite stupid."

Then after a slight pause:

"I am very close with the Italian Ambassador. Do
you think that if he intervened with the American Ambassador . . . ?"

"Such interventions have already been tried, unsuccessfully."

"Oh, what a pity! I shall have to wait."

At her request, the following Saturday, I accompanied
the Marquise de S——to the Steins.

Mlle. Gertrude Stein, because she was with some
friends, responded to our geeting by gesturing that we
were free to come and go.

M. Leo Stein was seated or rather sunk down in an

easy chair, his feet resting on the highest little end table in his library.

"Excellent for the digestion," he told me, making a small friendly sign.

When I recall these old times, I see again, on the walls of the Stein's apartment, the Matisses, the Picassos, and, by Cézanne, a portrait of Mme. Cézanne in gray on a red armchair. This canvas had belonged to me and I exhibited it at a retrospective of the Master of Aix organized at the *Salon d'Automne* of 1905. Since I often went to the exhibit, I had seen the Steins, the two brothers and their sister, seated on a bench in front of the portrait. They contemplated it silently until one day, after the Salon had closed, M. Leo Stein came to bring me the price of the canvas. He was accompanied by Mlle. Stein. "Now," she said, "the picture is ours." It had been stated as if the brother and sister had just paid the ransom for someone dear to them.

Mlle. Gertrude Stein had a complex personality. On seeing her dressed simply in her heavy corduroy clothing, her leather-thong sandals, one would think her a housewife whose horizon was bordered by her relations with the fruit seller, the dairyman, the spice dealer. But when her eyes met yours, one could see right away that there was in Mlle. Stein something more than the *bourgeoise.* The vivacity of her glance quickly showed her to be an observer whom nothing escaped. How could one not let oneself go, abandoning oneself completely, when one heard her laugh, a mocking laugh, as if she made fun of herself?

Recently someone said to me:

"I read, in the *Nouvelle Revue Française,* the description that Mlle. Stein just did of Matisse's studio. There isn't a single allusion to the painter's art. She simply notes the objects that she sees: a chair there,

an easel here; on the wall, an unframed picture; a statu-
ette on a console. . . ."

I pointed out to the speaker that one finds, under
the pen of Mlle. Stein, more than cold enumerations.
And, for example, even though I am unable to put a
name to a character in the most transparent *romans à
clef,* in a fragment of the memoirs of Mlle. Stein that
I have seen, would I not be recognized as that frown-
ing character who, at the threshold of his shop, his
two hands leaning on the door frame, looks at the
passers-by with the air of someone who wants to send
them to the devil? How often have I regretted not being
able to meet people in an easygoing, jovial way!

When I learned later that Mlle. Stein had engaged
as a translator a professor from the College of France,
M. Bernard Fay: "A professor from the College of
France," I noted to myself, "what will become of her!"
As far as translation goes, this is what happened to me.
I had written, in an article about Gauguin, that in
Tahiti he had suffered in his relationships with the
colonists. Then my translator:

"Why, M. Vollard, do you put 'colons' in the plural.
One only has one colon. The colon is part of the large
intestine." And seeing my bewilderment, he added,
"Don't worry, I looked it up in the dictionary."

NATALIE CLIFFORD BARNEY

Born in Dayton, Ohio, in 1877, Natalie Clifford Barney, heiress to a family fortune, fled to Europe in the early 1900s. Like Stein, who rejected the "uncompromising family likeness" of American women—their "conformity from within out"—Miss Barney was singularly uncomfortable in her homeland. "Yes the American girl is a crude virgin and she is safe in her freedom," Stein observed, concurring with Natalie Barney's scorn for her contemporaries.

In a three-hundred-year-old mansion on the rue Jacob, Miss Barney's salon rivaled Stein's in glamor. Paul Valéry, Colette, Remy de Gourmont were among the many who partook of the elegant chocolate cakes and fine liqueurs. At her frequent celebrations honoring *femmes de lettres* entertainment ranged from dramatic readings to startling spectacles. A bejeweled Mata Hari rode seminude through the garden and danced, fully naked, at a gathering for women only. After her morning horseback rides through the Bois de Boulogne, Miss Barney often assembled her friends in the garden's Grecian temple for a gracious tea.

Her salon was characterized by what Samuel Putnam called "dignified *abandon*," and the hostess herself was its most extraordinary figure. "She was charming," wrote Sylvia Beach, "and, all dressed in white and with her blond coloring, most attractive. Many of her sex found her fatally so, I believe."

Miss Barney made no attempt to conceal her lesbianism. Her flamboyant love affairs scandalized some, amused many, and inspired Sapphic poets and novelists.

A lifelong exile, Miss Barney became increasingly Parisian as the years passed. She wrote almost exclusively in French, recording her memories in five volumes spanning more than fifty years. Here she recalls the warmth and affection she felt for Gertrude Stein.

❦ *Natalie Clifford Barney / from Foreword to* As Fine As Melanctha

In recalling so magnetic a personality, how not, first of all, evoke this magnet to which so many adhered? For she attracted and influenced not only writers but painters, musicians, and least but not last, disciples. She used to declare "I don't mind meeting anyone once," but she rarely kept to so strict a limitation. Although the most affirmative person I ever met, she was a keen and responsive listener.

"Life is as others spoil it for us," concluded a beautiful friend of mine who had become a derelict through her fatalism. How many spoilt lives came to Gertrude with their misfortunes, due to some inextricable situation or sentimental rut? She, instead of offering helpless sympathy, often helped them out, by changing an *idée fixe* or obsession into a fresh start in a new direction.

As an appreciative pupil of William James, her study in reactions also proved salutary to the "spoilers" of lives. In these she sometimes detected a genius for deceit which she would aid them to confess, or she would indicate means to liberate them of their victims, since as Henry James—was it not?—wisely remarked, "There is only one thing worse than a tyrant and that is a tyrant's victim."

Even more interested in cases than in their cures, many served as characters in her plays and stories. Some of them may even discover themselves in this very book . . . that is, if they are sufficiently initiated into Miss Stein's game of blindman's buff, or blind-man's bluff, in which the reader is blindfolded—obscurity being the better part of discretion as to who is who. At other times she issued works of a most pene-trating and acute quality, filled with subtle analysis, like

Things As They Are.

Even I, who am not in the habit of consulting any-body about my dilemmas, once brought a problem of mine to the willing and experienced ear of Gertrude. In a moment, in a word, she diagnosed the complaint: "Consanguinity."

She never appeared to hesitate or reflect or take aim, but invariably hit the mark.

Our Walks

Often in the evening we would walk together; I, greeted at the door of 5 rue Christine by Gertrude's staunch presence, pleasant touch of hand, well-rounded voice always ready to chuckle. Our talks and walks led us far from war paths. For generally having no axe to grind nor anyone to execute with it, we felt detached and free to wander in our quiet old quarter where, while exercising her poodle, "Basket," we naturally fell into thought and step. Basket, unleashed, ran ahead, a white blur, the ghost of a dog in the moonlit side streets:

> Where ghosts and shadows mingle—
> As lovers, lost when single,

The night's enchantment made our conversation as light, iridescent and bouncing as soap bubbles, but as easily exploded when touched upon—so I'll touch on none of them for you, that a bubble may remain a bubble! And perhaps we never said *"d'impérissables choses."**

We also met during Gertrude Stein's lionized winter of 1934–35 in New York, and walked into one of its

*Baudelaire.

41

flashing, diamond-sharp days, where what one touches brings a spark to the finger tips.

Witnessing with apprehension Gertrude's independent crossing of streets without a qualm, I asked her why she never wavered on the edge of curbstones, as I did, with one foot forward and one foot backward, waiting for a propitious crowd and signal.

"All these people, including the nice taxi drivers, recognize and are careful of me." So saying, she set forth, her longish skirt flapping sail-like in a sea breeze, and landed across 59th Street in the park, as confidently as the Israélites over the isthmus of the Red Sea—while we, not daring to follow in her wake, risked being engulfed.

She accepted her fame as a tribute, long on the way but due, and enjoyed it thoroughly. Only once, in Paris—and indeed the last time I saw her—did the recognition of a cameraman displease her, for he waylaid her just as we were entering Rumpelmayer's patisserie. In order to satisfy her need for the cake, and the photographer's wish, she was photographed by him, through the plate-glass window, eating the chosen one. Her eagerness was partly caused by a disappointing lunch we had just experienced at Prunier's, where each sort of sea food we ordered—prompted by appetites accrued by our recent wartime privations and still existing restrictions—was denied us, until at last (this was in 1946), driven to despair of a bettered world, Gertrude dropped her head between her hands and shook it from side to side; and not until we reached that rue de Rivoli patisserie did her spirits and appetite revive and meet with a partial compensation.

Their Cakes

The discovery of cakes had always been a peacetime pursuit of Gertrude and Alice. Meeting them by chance at Aix-le-Bains, I enquired why they happened

to be on this opposite bank of the Lac du Bourget, and
was informed of a new sort of cake created in one of the
villages on a mountain beyond. But first obliged to
go on other errands, they descended from the lofty seat
of their old Ford car—Alice bejeweled as an idol and
Gertrude with the air of an Indian divinity. As they
disappeared around a corner, not without causing won-
derment, the only appropriate offering seemed to me one
of those long, hose-stemmed lotus flowers of dark pink,
which I purchased and stuck between the spokes of
Gertrude's steering wheel, with a card of explanation:
"A wand to lead you on."

Another meeting with this inseparable couple took
place in their *jardin de cure* at Bilignin, on another
summer afternoon. It somewhat resembled the dust
jacket Cecil Beaton designed for Gertrude Stein's *Wars
I Have Seen,* only a huge parasol replaced the para-
chutes and we sat peacefully on gaily striped canvas
chairs. The four of us—for Romaine Brooks had come
along with me—and Basket, all curves and capers, lent
a circus effect to the scene. As China tea was being
served, Alice placed on the round outdoor table a
fluffy confection of hers, probably a coconut layer
cake which only Americans know how to make—and
eat. Its white icing, edged with ornamental pink,
matched Basket's like coating and incidental pinks.
Gertrude sat in the favorite position in which Picasso
portrayed her, clothed in rough attire, with moccasined
feet, knees far apart, reminiscent of the gypsy-queen
under her tent in my old Bar Harbor days.

Meanwhile Romaine, contemplating our group and
finding it "paintable," wished to start a picture of it
then and there, before the light or her inspiration should
fade. But I, the disturbing element of the party, because
of a clock in my mind and in duty bound to pleasures,
insisted that Romaine and I were due elsewhere. So
this picture of us was left unpainted: *mea culpa!*

Gertrude's and Alice's flair for cakes makes me conclude that while poets are left to starve in garrets —or, as here in France, in *chambres de bonnes*—living only in the past and future, with the hope of an aftermath of fame, an author such as Gertrude Stein, admitting of nothing but a "continuous present," must be sustained on sweetmeats and timely success, this being the surest way of taking the cake and of eating and having it too.

Faith in Herself

Her belief in herself never failed her. Even when still a child, she and her brother Leo used to discuss who would prove to be their family's genius. Leo thought himself that predestined genius; but Gertrude, turning to us—her two visitors were that afternoon Madame de Clermont-Tonnerre and myself—emphatically declared: "But, as you know, it turned out to be me!"

Indeed, such a faith in oneself "passeth understanding," and what a poor thing is understanding, compared to such a faith!

As faith is far more exalting than reason, she once deplored Ezra Pound's becoming "the village explainer," which led so great a poet, and discoverer of poets, to his present standstill.

Her Lecture at Oxford

From the crest of Gertrude Stein's tidal wave of success, she was persuaded by Harold Acton to lecture to a class of students at Oxford University, and she managed to hold them spellbound without a single concession to meet their understanding. Her lecture soared above their heads as they sensed something that surpassed them, but which freed neither their laughter nor their judgment, so that nothing was left to them but to applaud uproariously.

She afterwards consented to meet them on their level

and both their questions and her answers were reported, inspiring and inspired.

With Our G.I.s

This same democratic spirit made her popular with our G.I.s of the Second World War. They also gathered something unique from her presence amongst them, and so she led them, as a sort of *vivandière de l'esprit,* from war into peace, and to realize their own, instead of their collective, existence. But in some cases this change was hard to bring about, loath as they were to be "separated from," no longer "club together, be part of, belong to," etc. This fact was brought even to my notice in Florence by a big G.I. who confessed to me that "the urge to join his comrades was so strong he couldn't even stop a moment to brush his teeth"! The disbanding of the herd instinct—to rebecome individual and perhaps a nobody instead of a company, to be left to the responsibility of oneself instead of leaving it to a chief in command with everything settled for you (death included), to take off a uniform to become uniform—all this was more than some of them could stand.

And how not to feel homesick for their regiment when forced homeward, perhaps to intrude on a family, or face hostile businessmen? At such a moment Gertrude Stein met them with her invigorating affirmations and cheered them on.

It must have been about this period that she was photographed against our Stars and Stripes.

Becoming Singular

Patriotic as Gertrude Stein seemed, she certainly dispelled our discouraging axiom that "one man's as good as another." No one has ever dared to say this of the American woman!

From her *Making of Americans,* I translated into French some of her most significant pages on our "progress in becoming singular." These pages were read —between wars—in my salon, at meetings destined to bring about a better *entente* between French, English, and American authors.

On my "Friday" celebrating Gertrude Stein, Mina Loy addressed them by explaining her admiration for this innovator who "swept the literary circus clear for future performances."

Many examples, including her own, were read to this effect—and a zeal for translating seized upon many of us from then on.

My *Aventures de L'esprit,* published in 1929, mentions these reunions as well as my literary adventures, including letters to me from Pierre Louÿs, Gabriel d'Annunzio, Marcel Proust, Rilke, Max Jacob, Paul Valéry, etc. This book Gertrude wanted to see translated for America, for it gives an incomplete but authentic résumé of our best period, and of those who made it so—and Gertrude Stein was included in this period and the forming of her own. How she stood her ground, never (unless to influence or appreciate) infringing on the ground of others. Indeed she made no allowances that "he who runs may read," and was heedless whether, having read, he ran.

We doubt if she ever thought of her readers at all.

In going over my impressions of her—*de vive voix, de vive mémoire*—in these fragmentary evidences, I find that I have somewhat replaced the essential by the superficial. I suppose that to want to enjoy and know such a personage without going into her more original ambitions and works is like seizing chance reflections from a water-mirror regardless of its depth; this is what I find myself doing here, and avoiding the significance of her undersea mysteries. Yet I have tried to dive deeper, and only touched rock bottom to be ejected up again to the surface, suffocating with too much salt water, in search of too rare a pearl.

CARL VAN VECHTEN

Gertrude Stein first glimpsed Carl Van Vechten at the second performance of Stravinsky's *Sacre du Printemps,* in 1913. He was "a tall well built young man," she noted, "and he wore a soft evening shirt with the tiniest pleats all over the front of it." Struck by his elegant appearance, she returned home and immediately wrote a portrait of him called, simply, "One."

Van Vechten was equally impressed a few days later when he called on Gertrude Stein at her home. Of all her admirers, he was the one who most directly led her to fame, and she acknowledged his role in *The Autobiography of Alice B. Toklas:*

> In season and out he kept her name and her work before the public. When he was beginning to be well known and they asked him what he thought the most important book of the year he replied *Three Lives* by Gertrude Stein. His loyalty and his effort never weakened.

He was born in Cedar Rapids, Iowa, in 1880. "You are brilliant and subtle if you come from Iowa," Gertrude Stein remarked. But for Van Vechten, Iowa offered nothing but bland middle-class complacency; he escaped as early as he could, enrolling at the University of Chicago and staying on in the city after he graduated in 1903. For the next three years he held a minor job on the staff of the *Chicago American*, spending as much time as he could in the city's theaters and concert halls. Although Chicago was a step beyond Cedar Rapids, it was not New York. In the spring of 1906 he headed East.

His career as a writer on the arts began with a position as assistant music critic for the *New York Times*, and he approached the task with tireless enthusiasm. He was writing for the *New York Press* and contributing to the *Trend* (where this selection originally appeared) when he met Stein during a visit to Paris. By 1922 he had turned novelist, fictionalizing his experiences in Paris and Greenwich Village in *Peter Whiffle: His Life and Works*, which received praise from Elinor Wylie, Carl Van Doren—and of course Stein—and sold surprisingly well.

Throughout his years as a writer Van Vechten spurred the acceptance of such novelists as Faulkner and Ronald Firbank, then considered avant-garde. He was among the first established critics to recognize the renaissance in Negro arts and literature that was flourishing in Harlem, and he actively helped to establish the careers of Countee Cullen, Langston Hughes, James Weldon Johnson, Bessie Smith, and Ethel Waters.

Though much of his writing on Negro arts appeared in *Vanity Fair*, he attempted a larger statement—one he hoped would bring the races closer together—in a novel he unfortunately titled *Nigger Heaven*. Gertrude Stein wrote enthusiastically that she found it "delicate and real. . . . I am awfully pleased that it is so good." She shared his belief that the only "pioneering" being done in America was being done by Negroes. But others were not as kind as she. The book was attacked by both races, stirring up passions Van Vechten had not foreseen.

Yet the novel did not diminish his stature as a critic, and his efforts on behalf of Gertrude Stein continued to be taken seriously. He acted as her agent in America, persuading Bennett Cerf that Random House should become her exclusive American publisher. He arranged her 1934 lecture tour, attending to every detail for her comfort. He met her boat, arranged for her hotel suite, accompanied her on her first flight (she wouldn't fly without him), set up a small private lecture so she could get used to speaking before a group. Above all, he never failed in his support. She called him the Patriarch, and he replied, "it makes me feel like Moses or Abraham, but I guess I did lead you into the Promised Land. . . ."

Van Vechten capped his long career in the arts by turning from writing to photography. From 1932 on his subjects ranged from Robinson Jeffers to Edna St. Vincent Millay, Tallulah Bankhead to Thomas Mann. During Stein's tour he brought her to his fifty-fifth Street apartment in New York to do a portrait of her. According to Alice Toklas, he took hundreds of photographs of Stein.

Stein named Van Vechten her literary executor, asking that he arrange for all her works to be published eventually. With Thornton Wilder, he saw that her papers were deposited safely at Yale, and the seventh and final volume of her writing was published by Yale University Press in 1957 under his guidance.* "I always wanted to be historical, from almost a baby on, I felt that way about it," Stein admitted shortly before she died, "and Carl was one of the earliest ones that made me be certain that I was going to be."

---

*Two additional volumes of previously uncollected material have been brought out by Black Sparrow Press (1974), edited by Robert Bartlett Haas: *Reflection on the Atomic Bomb* and *How Writing Is Written.*

🌺 Carl Van Vechten / "How To
Read Gertrude Stein"

What is there to say for Gertrude Stein that she does not say quite adequately for herself? Is it not clear that her effect is made on all her readers? True, the effect varies, but did two people ever feel the same about Beethoven's Ninth Symphony? Why, even at the present moment the *Evening Globe* is being bombarded with letters from people who prefer "Put on Your Old Gray Bonnet" to the masterpiece of the Bonn composer. Yet Beethoven's Ninth Symphony, even in the people that it does not reach as a solace and a boon, stirs a vague unrest, a feeling of reproach or of discontent.

"There is an art that we do not understand."

It seems unnecessary to go so far afield as Beethoven in the beginning of an article concerning Miss Stein's *Tender Buttons*. Perhaps it is sufficient to send forth at first the mere suggestion that Miss Stein has added enormously to the vagueness of the English language, and vagueness is a quality that belongs to the English language, just as buildings on the Riviera sigh to be painted white, so that in the glory of that Southern sun they may reflect a thousand colors.

The English language is a language of hypocrisy and evasion. How not to say a thing has been the problem of our writers from the earliest times. The extraordinary fluidity and even naïveté of French makes it possible for a writer in that language to babble like a child; de Maupassant is only possible in French, a language in which the phrase *"Je t' aime"* means everything. But what does "I love you" mean in English? Donald Evans, one of our poets, has realized this peculiar quality of English and he is almost the first of the poets in English to say unsuspected and revolting things, because he so cleverly avoids saying them.

Miss Stein discovered the method before Mr. Evans. In fact his Patagonian Sonnets were an offshoot of her later manner, just as Miss Kenton's superb story, "Nicknames," derives its style from Miss Stein's *Three Lives*. She has really turned language into music, really made its sound more important than its sense. And she has suggested to the reader a thousand channels for his mind and sense to drift along, a thousand instead of a stupid only one.

Miss Stein has no explanations to offer regarding her work. I have often questioned her, but I have met with no satisfaction. She asks you to read. Her intimate connection with the studies of William James have been commented upon; some say "the fringe of thought," so frequently referred to by that writer, may dominate her working consciousness. Her method of work is unique. She usually writes in the morning, and she sets down the words as they come from her pen; they bubble, they flow; they surge through her brain and she sets them down. You may regard them as nonsense, but the fact remains that effective imitations of her style do not exist. John Reed tells me that, while he finds her stimulating and interesting, an entity, he feels compelled to regard her work as an offshoot, something that will not be concluded by followers. She lives and dies alone, a unique example of a strange art. It may be in place also to set down here the fact that once in answer to a question Miss Stein asserted that her art was for the printed page only; she never expects people to converse or exchange ideas in her style.

As a personality Gertrude Stein is unique. She is massive in physique, a Rabelaisian woman with a splendid thoughtful face; mind dominating her matter. Her velvet robes, mostly brown, and her carpet slippers associate themselves with her indoor appearance. To go out she belts herself, adds a walking staff, and a trim unmodish turban. This garb suffices for a shopping tour or a box party at the Opéra.

Paris is her abode. She settled there after Cambridge, and association with William James, Johns Hopkins and a study of medicine. Her orderly mind has captured the scientific facts of both psychology and physiology. And in Paris the early painters of the new era captured her heart and purse. She purchased the best of them, and now such examples as Picasso's *Acrobats* and early Matisses hang on her walls. There is also the really authoritative portrait of herself, painted by Pablo Picasso.

These two painters she lists among her great friends. And their influence, perhaps, decided her in her present mode of writing. Her pictures are numerous, and to many, who do not know of her as a writer, she is mentioned as the Miss Stein with the collection of post-impressionists. On Saturday nights during the winter one can secure a card of admission to the collection and people wander in and out the studio, while Miss Stein serves her dinner guests unconcernedly with after-dinner coffee. And conversation continues, strangely unhindered by the picture viewers.

Leo Stein happens in, when he is not in Florence, and I have a fancy that he prefers Florence to Paris. He is her brother, and their tastes in art are naturally antithetical. He believes in the painters of the "third dimension," the painters of atmosphere, and the space between objects, for thus he describes the impressionists, and he includes Peter Paul Rubens in this group. And his precise manner of grouping thought is strangely at odds with Miss Stein's piquant love of gossip, and with her strange undercurrents of ideas that pass from her through and about the place.

Mr. Stein's phrase "Define what you mean by—" is almost famous. It is well known wherever he appears. Last I saw him in the Piazza Vittorio Emanuele. I sat at luncheon time on the terrace of the Giubbi Rossi with Mabel Dodge when he strode into view, sandals on his feet, a bundle over his shoulder, and carrying an alpenstock. He was on his way to the mountains, and, if I remember rightly, he asked me, in response to an invitation, to define what I meant by "cocktail," something singularly difficult to do in Italy.

Miss Stein's presence, as I have said before my parenthesis, is strangely dominant in these evenings and her clear deep voice, her very mellow laugh, the adjunct of an almost abnormal sense of humor and observation, remain very pleasant memories. At one time I saw her very frequently, but we talked little of her work, although we often read it.

Of all her books only *Tender Buttons,* the latest of them to appear, is generally procurable. Besides this I know of *Three Lives,* written in her early manner; *Portrait of Mabel Dodge at the Villa Curonia,* an internationally famous monograph, published privately in Florence, and never on sale. There is a very long autobiographical work, at present, I believe considerably longer than *Clarissa Harlowe,* which runs through her various changes of style. There are several plays, one about me, which Miss Stein very kindly entitled "One." These are very short and in her very late manner. Miss Florence Bradley wished to play them in America and she may have done so in Chicago. She is now on her way to China and she may play them there; but I have no record of performances. Miss Stein is most insistent that they be performed before they are printed, but she did allow Marsden Hartley to quote from a play about him as a foreword to his collection of pictures which was exhibited at that "little place" of Mr. Stieglitz's at 291 Fifth Avenue. There are several other short portraits, and some sketches, one of shop girls in the Gallerie Lafayette in Paris which is particularly descriptive and amusing. These, I think, are Miss Stein's main contributions to her complete works.

In *Three Lives* Miss Stein attained at a bound an amount of literary facility which a writer might strive in vain for years to acquire. Simplicity is a quality one is born with, so far as literary style is concerned, and Miss Stein was born with that. But to it she added, in this work, a vivid note of reiteration, a fascinatingly complete sense of psychology and the workings of minds one on the other, which at least in "Melanctha: Each as She May" reaches a state of perfection which might have satisfied such masters of craft as Turgenev, or Balzac, or Henry James.

Quotation from this book is difficult. I shall quote a very short paragraph to give a sense of the style, and to show that those who are afraid of this writer in her present form need not be afraid of *Three Lives*.

"Jeff did not like it very well these days, in his true feeling. He knew now very well Melanctha was not strong enough inside her to stand any more of his slow way of doing. And yet now he knew he was not honest in his feeling. Now he always had to show more to Melanctha than he was ever feeling. Now she made him go so fast, and he knew it was not real with his feeling, and yet he could not make her suffer so any more because he always was so slow with his feeling."

The story, it may be added, is about Negroes, and it is as poignant in its material as it is in its use of it. The book was published by the Grafton Press in New York. I think it is now out of print, but stray copies may sometimes be secured from dealers in rare books.

The number of *Camera Work* for August, 1912, contains two articles by Miss Stein about her two friends,

Henri Matisse and Pablo Picasso. To me they seem to bridge the period between *Three Lives* and *Portrait of Mabel Dodge at the Villa Curonia.*

These have been considerably quoted in derision by newspaper paragraphers, but they are admirable examples of the effect of reiteration and of intertwining of ideas and phrases in style. Here is a quotation:

"This one was one having always something being coming out of him, something having completely a real meaning. This one was one whom some were following. This one was one who was working. This one was one who was working and he was one needing this thing needing to be working so as to be one having some way of working. This one was one who was working."

Portrait of Mabel Dodge at the Villa Curonia made a winter amusing for those who subscribed to the clipping bureaus. The redoubtable Romeike, whom Whistler mentions, was kept busy cutting out ideas of the scriveners in Oshkosh and Flatbush about Miss Stein. To those who know Mrs. Dodge the portrait may seem to be a true one; it has intention, that is even obvious to those who do not know what the intention is. There is nothing faint or pale about Miss Stein's authority. It is as complete in its way as the authority of Milton. You may not like the words, but you are forced to admit, after, perhaps, a struggle that no other words will do.

For the sake of the few benighted ones who have not had this work quoted to them I offer the following passage, which is quite as familiar, I should say, as Wordsworth's "A primrose at the river's brim."

"A bottle that has all the time to stand open is not so clearly shown when there is green colour there. This is not the only way to change it. A little raw potato and then all that softer does happen to show that there has been enough. It changes the expression."

And now a discussion of *Tender Buttons* seems im-

minent. Donald Evans, who is responsible for its
publication, says that it is the only book ever printed
which contains absolutely no errors. I have not Miss
Stein's authority for this statement. At any rate the
effect on printers and proofreaders was tremendous. I
believe that even yet some of them are suffering from
brain storm. *Portrait of Mabel Dodge at the Villa
Curonia,* was set up in Florence by compositors who,
I believe, did not read English. So their trouble was less.

There are several theories extant relating to *Tender
Buttons.* I may say that one I upheld stoutly for a few
hours, that the entire book has a physical application,
I have since rejected, at least in part. The three divisions
which comprise the books in a way explain the title.
They are "Food; Objects; Rooms," all things which
fasten our lives together, and whose complications may
be said to make them "tender."

The majestic rhythm of the prose in this book; the
virtuosity with which Miss Stein intertwines her words,
are qualities which strike the ear at once. And *Tender
Buttons* benefits by reading aloud. Onomatopoeia,
sound echoing sense, is a favorite figure of speech with
Miss Stein; so is alliteration which is fatally fascinating
when mingled with reiteration, and Miss Stein drops
repeated words upon your brain with the effect of
Chopin's B Minor Prelude, which is popularly supposed
to represent the raindrops falling on the roof at Majorca
on one of those George Sand days.

The mere sensuous effect of the words is irresistible
and often as in the section labeled "Eating," or "A
Seltzer Bottle," the mere pronunciation of words gives
the effect of the act or the article. On the other hand,
"A Little Called Pauline," seems to me perfect in the
way of a pretty description, a Japanese print of a
charming creature. "Suppose an Eyes" is similarly a
picture, but more postery.

It would seem to me that the inspiration offered to

writers in this book was an enormous incentive to read it. What writer after reading *Tender Buttons* but would strive for a fresher phrase, a more perfect rhythmic prose? Gertrude Stein to me is one of the supreme stylists.

In case one is not delighted, amused, or appealed to in any way by the sensuous charm of her art then, of course, there is the sense to fall back on; the ideas expressed. Here one floats about vaguely for a key to describe how to tell what Miss Stein means. Her vagueness is innate and one of her most positive qualities. I have already said how much she adds to language by it. You may get the idea of it if you close your eyes and imagine yourself awaking from the influence of ether, as you gasp to recall some words or ideas, while new ones surge into your brain. A certain sleepy consciousness. Or you may read sense through the figures as they flit rapidly—almost word by word—through your brain. It is worthy of note that almost everyone tries to make sense out of Miss Stein just as everyone insists on making photographs out of drawings by Picabia, when the essential of his art is that he is getting away from the photographic.

And now for a few quotations from *Tender Buttons*:

"RED ROSES: A cool red rose and a pink cut pink, a collapse and a solid hole, a little less hot."

"A SOUND: Elephant beaten with candy and little pops and chews all bolts and reckless reckless rats, this is this."

Roast beef is Miss Stein's favorite food and she has devoted nearly seven pages in the section labeled "Food" to its delights, while oranges and such-like are let off with single phrases. In the middle of the description of roast beef is a verse, discovered for me by Neith Boyce, which I print in verse form, although it is not disclosed in the book:

> Lovely snipe and tender turn,
> Excellent vapor and slender butter
> All the splinter and the trunk,
> All the poisonous darning drunk,
> All the joy in weak success,
> All the joyful tenderness,
> All the section and the tea,
> All the stouter symmetry.

Celery is thus described: "Celery tastes tastes where in curled lashes and little bits and mostly in remains."

"A green acre is so selfish and so pure and so enlivened."

And the description of chicken has already become a byword among certain groups of those who love bywords:

"Alas a dirty word, alas a dirty third alas a dirty third, alas a dirty bird."

SYLVIA BEACH

The daughter of a Presbyterian minister from Princeton, New Jersey, Sylvia Beach came to Paris in 1917 to pursue her interest in contemporary French writing. For a while she lived with her beautiful sister, Cyprian, an actress, in a "fairly respectable" quarter near the Palais Royal. Her search for current literature soon brought her to *La Maison des Amis des Livres,* run by Adrienne Monnier. The bookshop was a popular rendezvous for French writers, a salon where hundreds gathered to listen to André Gide read the poems of Paul Valéry or hear Valéry Larbaud read his translation of *Ulysses,* or to attend an occasional musical program by Erik Satie or Francis Poulenc.

Miss Beach and Mlle. Monnier, sharing a love of literature, became close friends, making as odd a couple as Gertrude Stein and Alice Toklas. Large, buxom Mlle. Monnier, who reminded Virgil Thomson of "a French milkmaid from the eighteenth century," contrasted with Miss Beach's pert boyishness. "Angular Sylvia, in her box-like suits, was Alice in Wonderland at forty," Thomson recalled.

Sylvia Beach had long wanted to open a bookshop of her own, and now began to plan a French shop in New York, where she could make known the works of the new French writers introduced to her by Adrienne Monnier. When it became apparent, however, that the costs of establishing a shop in America would be too high, she was forced to abandon her dream.

Mlle. Monnier, delighted to keep her friend in Paris, suggested that instead of a French bookstore in New York, she open an American shop near *La Maison des Amis des Livres*. Quickly convinced, Sylvia Beach sent a telegram to her mother in Princeton, saying simply: "Opening bookshop in Paris. Please send money." Mrs. Beach forwarded her entire savings.

On November 19, 1919, Shakespeare and Company took down its shutters for the first time. Photographs of Walt Whitman and Edgar Allan Poe hung beside two drawings by William Blake; some Whitman manuscripts —family heirlooms—were carefully displayed among the flea-market furnishings and the varied selection of English and American books. Within hours the first customers arrived—among them André Gide and André Maurois—and for more than twenty years, Miss Beach recalled, "they never gave me time to meditate."

Miss Beach's cheerful friendliness welcomed many newly arrived Americans to Paris. Hemingway remembered her "lively, sharply sculptured face, brown eyes that were alive as a small animal's and as gay as a young girl's, and wavy brown hair." She let him borrow books without paying the required rental fee, and often gently reminded him to eat. "No one that I ever knew was nicer to me," he said years later.

The shop served not only as a meeting place but even as a mailing address. Robert McAlmon's publishing house, Contact Editions, received manuscripts and orders c/o Shakespeare and Company, and it was a rare day that the blue-eyed young writer did not wander in once or twice.* He was part of "the Crowd," the writers and

*Robert McAlmon—poet, writer, publisher and editor— established and co-edited the journal *Contact* with William Carlos Williams in New York. Transplanted to Paris, the

artists whose portraits, photographed by Man Ray or Berenice Abbott, gradually filled the walls beside the Blake drawings.

Among Miss Beach's customers was James Joyce, who would borrow dozens of books and keep them for years. He sat quietly for hours at a time in the shadowy corner of the shop, emerging only rarely to be introduced to an aspiring writer. In 1922, Shakespeare and Company dared to publish his *Ulysses,* selling it by subscription throughout Europe and Great Britain and making literary history.

Since Gertrude Stein's studio was just a few blocks from the rue de l'Odéon where Shakespeare and Company finally settled, she and Miss Toklas were frequent visitors. In turn, Sylvia Beach often brought young writers—Sherwood Anderson among them—to the rue de Fleurus to meet the legendary writer.

---

journal evolved into a publishing house whose authors included Hemingway, Hilda Doolittle, Ezra Pound, Dorothy Richardson, and Bryher (then McAlmon's wife). In 1925 Contact Editions published 505 copies of Stein's *The Making of Americans.*

❧ *Sylvia Beach / from*
Shakespeare and Company

Not long after I had opened my bookshop, two
women came walking down the rue Dupuytren. One of
them, with a very fine face, was stout, wore a long
robe, and, on her head, a most becoming top of a
basket. She was accompanied by a slim, dark, whimsical
woman: she reminded me of a gipsy. They were
Gertrude Stein and Alice B. Toklas.

Having been an early reader of *Tender Buttons* and
Three Lives, I was, of course, very joyful over my new
customers. And I enjoyed their continual banter.
Gertrude was always teasing me about my bookselling,
which appeared to amuse her considerably. It amused
me, too.

Her remarks and those of Alice, which rounded them
out, were inseparable. Obviously they saw things from
the same angle, as people do when they are perfectly
congenial. Their two characters, however, seemed to me
quite independent of each other. Alice had a great deal
more finesse than Gertrude. And she was grown up:
Gertrude was a child, something of an infant prodigy.

Gertrude subscribed to my lending library, but complained that there were no amusing books in it. Where,
she asked indignantly, were those American masterpieces *The Trail of the Lonesome Pine* and *A Girl of
the Limberlost?* This was humiliating for the librarian.
I produced the works of Gertrude Stein, all I had been
able to lay my hands on at the time, and I wondered
if she could mention another library in Paris that had

two copies of *Tender Buttons* circulating. To make up
for her unjust criticism of Shakespeare and Company,
she bestowed several of her works on us: quite rare
items such as *Portrait of Mabel Dodge at the Villa
Curonia* and that thing with the terrifying title, *Have
They Attacked Mary. He giggled. A Political Caricature.* Also the special number of the Stieglitz publication, *Camera Work,* containing her pieces on Picasso
and Matisse. But, above all, I valued the copy of
Melanctha in the first edition, which Gertrude inscribed
for me. I should have locked it up; someone stole it
from the bookshop.

Gertrude's subscription was merely a friendly gesture. She took little interest, of course, in any but her
own books. But she did write a poem about my bookshop, which she brought to me one day in 1920. It was
entitled "Rich and Poor in English" and bore the subtitle, "to subscribe in French and other Latin Tongues."
You can find it in *Painted Lace,* Volume V of the Yale
edition of her work.

I saw Gertrude and Alice often. Either they dropped
in to observe my bookselling business or I went around
to their *pavillon* in the rue de Fleurus near the Luxembourg Gardens. It was at the back of the court. Gertrude alway lay stretched on a divan and always joked
and teased. The *pavillon* was as fascinating as its
occupants. On its walls were all those wonderful
Picassos of the "Blue period." Also, Gertrude showed
me the albums that contained his drawings, of which
she had collected a good many. She told me that she
and her brother Leo had agreed to divide between them
all the pictures they possessed. He had chosen Matisse,
she Picasso. I remember some paintings by Juan Gris,
too.

Once, Gertrude and Alice took me for a ride into the
country. They drove up noisily in the old Ford named
Gody, a veteran of the war and companion in their war

work. Gertrude showed me Gody's latest acquisitions—
headlights that could be turned on and off at will from
inside the car and an electric cigarette lighter. Gertrude
smoked continuously. I climbed up on the high seat beside Gertrude and Alice, and off we roared to Mildred
Aldrich's "hilltop on the Marne." Gertrude did the driving, and presently, when a tire blew out, she did the
mending. Very competently too, while Alice and I
chatted by the roadside.

Gertrude Stein's admirers, until they had met her and
discovered how affable she was, were often "skeered"
to approach her without proper protection. So the poor
things would come to me, exactly as if I were a guide
from one of the tourist agencies, and beg me to take
them to see Gertrude Stein.

My tours, arranged with Gertrude and Alice before-
hand, took place in the evenings. They were cheerfully
endured by the ladies in the *pavillon,* who were always
cordial and hospitable.

One of the first of these tourists was a young friend
of mine who hung around Shakespeare and Company a
great deal in 1919–20, Stephen Benét. He may be seen
in one of the first press photos of the bookshop, that
fellow peering through his glasses at a book and very
serious-looking compared with my sister Holly and me
in the back of the shop.

At his request, and on his own responsibility, I took
Stephen to see Gertrude Stein. This was before his
marriage to that charming Rosemary, whom he later
brought to the bookshop. The visit to Gertrude went off
pleasantly. I believe Stephen mentioned that he had
some Spanish blood, and since Gertrude and Alice liked
anything Spanish, that interested them. I don't think the
meeting left any traces, however.

Another "tourist" who asked me to take him around
to the rue de Fleurus was Sherwood Anderson. One day
I noticed an interesting-looking man lingering on the

doorstep, his eye caught by a book in the window. The book was *Winesburg, Ohio,* which had recently been published in the United States. Presently he came in and introduced himself as the author. He said he hadn't seen another copy of his book in Paris. I was not surprised, as I had looked everywhere for it myself—in one place they had said, "Anderson, Anderson? Oh, sorry, we have only the Fairy Tales."

Sherwood Anderson was full of something that had happened to him, a step he had taken, a decision he had made that was of the greatest importance in his life. I listened with suspense to the story of how he had suddenly abandoned his home and a prosperous paint business, had simply walked away one morning, shaking off forever the fetters of respectability and the burden of security.

Anderson was a man of great charm, and I became very fond of him. I saw him as a mixture of poet and evangelist (without the preaching), with perhaps a touch of the actor. Anyhow, he was a most interesting man. . . .

Sherwood told me that Gertrude Stein's writing had influenced him. He admired her immensely, and asked me if I would introduce him to her. I knew he needed no introduction, but I gladly consented to conduct him to the rue de Fleurus.

This meeting was something of an event. Sherwood's deference and the admiration he expressed for her writing pleased Gertrude immensely. She was visibly touched. Sherwood's wife, Tennessee, who had accompanied us, didn't fare so well. She tried in vain to take part in the interesting conversation between the two writers, but Alice held her off. I knew the rules and regulations about wives at Gertrude's. They couldn't be kept from coming, but Alice had strict orders to keep them out of the way while Gertrude conversed with the husbands. Tennessee was less tractable than most. She seated herself on a table ready to take part in the conversation, and resisted when Alice offered to show her something on the right side of the sitting room. But Tennessee never succeeded in hearing a word of what they were saying. I pitied the thwarted lady—I couldn't see the necessity for the cruelty to wives that was practiced in the rue de Fleurus. Still, I couldn't help being amused at Alice's wife-proof technique. Curiously, it was only applied to wives; non-wives were admitted to Gertrude's conversation.

Sherwood Anderson was judged harshly by the young writers; and suffered considerably from the falling-off of his followers. But he was a forerunner, and, whether they acknowledge it or not, the generation of the twenties owes him a considerable debt.

Gertrude Stein had so much charm that she could often, though not always, get away with the most monstrous absurdities, which she uttered with a certain childish malice. Her aim was usually to tease somebody; nothing amused her as much. Adrienne Monnier, whom I took around to Gertrude's once, didn't find her very amusing. "You French," Gertrude declared, "have no Alps in literature, no Shakespeare; all your genius is in those speeches of the generals: fanfare. Such as *'On ne passera pas!'* "

I disagreed with Gertrude on French writing as well as on other writing, for instance, Joyce's. She was disappointed in me when I published *Ulysses;* she even came with Alice to my bookshop to announce that they had transferred their membership to the American Library on the Right Bank. I was sorry, of course, to lose two customers all of a sudden, but one mustn't coerce them. In the rue de l'Odéon, I must admit, we kept low company.

Thus "The Flowers of Friendship Faded Friendship Faded," at least for a time. But resentment fades as well. It's so difficult to remember exactly what a disagreement was all about. And there was Gertrude Stein's writing; nothing could affect my enjoyment of that.

After a while, I saw Gertrude and Alice again. They came to see whether I had anything by William Dean Howells, a major American writer, according to Gertrude, and unjustly neglected. I had his complete works, and made Gertrude and Alice take them all home.

Toward the end of 1930, I went one day with Joyce to a party at the studio of our friend Jo Davidson. Gertrude Stein, a fellow-bust of Joyce's, was also there. They had never met, so, with their mutual consent, I introduced them to each other and saw them shake hands quite peacefully.

Dear Jo Davidson! How we did miss him when he was gone.

The last time I took a "skeered" person to see Gertrude was when Ernest Hemingway told me he wanted to make up his quarrel with her but couldn't get up the courage to go alone. I encouraged him in his plan, and promised to accompany him to the rue Christine, where Gertrude and Alice were then living. I thought it better for Hemingway to go up alone, so I took him all the way to her door and left him with my best wishes. He came to tell me afterward that it was "fine" between them again.

Wars between writers blaze up frequently, but I have observed that they settle down eventually into smudges.

SHERWOOD ANDERSON

In 1914, seven years before he met Gertrude Stein, Sherwood Anderson discovered her recently published volume, *Tender Buttons,* that slim collection of descriptions of such everyday objects as a box, a plate, a seltzer bottle, a book, an apple. But the descriptions themselves, far from ordinary, are whimsical, unexpected, and, to some, unintelligible. To Sherwood Anderson, *Tender Buttons* opened a new dimension in language.

It excited me as one might grow excited in going in a new and wonderful country where everything is strange—a sort of Lewis and Clark expedition for me. Here words laid before me as the painter had laid the color pans on the table in my presence. My mind did a kind of jerking flop and after Miss Stein's book had come into my hands I spent days going about with a tablet of paper in my pocket and making new and strange combinations of words. The result was I thought a new familiarity with the words of my own vocabulary. I became a little conscious where before I had been unconscious. Perhaps it was then I really fell in love with words, wanted to give each word I used every chance to show itself at its best.

Tender Buttons, as Anderson so aptly understood,

"was something purely experimental and dealing in words separated from sense—in the ordinary meaning of the word sense—an approach I was sure the poets must often be compelled to make." It was an approach he decided to try. He would aim, as Miss Stein explained in *Portraits and Repetition*, "to express what something was, a little by talking and listening to that thing, but a great deal by looking at that thing."

A table, for her, took on a new aura:
A table means does it not my dear it means a whole steadiness. Is it likely that a change.

A table means more than a glass even a looking glass is tall. A table means necessary places and a revision a revision of a little thing it means it does mean that there has been a stand, a stand where it did shake.

Anderson, though, never took up Miss Stein's style. *Tender Buttons* and her other works, especially *Three Lives*, enabled him to find another kind of liberation. He wrote of Stein to his daughter-in-law in 1934:

She taught me to recognize the second person in myself, the poet-writing person, so that I could occasionally release that one.
And not blame it for the anxious person, myself as known by others.
You can see the great gain in that to me and why I think Stein is a genius.

When Sherwood Anderson finally arrived in Paris in 1921, he asked Sylvia Beach to arrange for him to visit Gertrude Stein in her rue de Fleurus studio, and, as Stein recalled, "quite simply and directly as was his way told her what he thought of her work and what it had meant to him in his development." Other writers had taken Stein as mentor, absorbed what they would, and then, disappointingly for her, strayed in their loyalty and affection. But Anderson remained an out-spoken defender of her art, acknowledging in print what he often expressed to her—his debt, his gratitude, his esteem.

"You always manage to say so much and say it straighter than anyone else I know," he wrote of her comments on *A Story Teller's Story,* his autobiography. And he readily admitted, "It was a vital day for me when I stumbled upon you."

Their friendship flourished for twenty years, until Anderson died in 1941, and with him the plans for a joint work on Ulysses S. Grant, their "great American hero." Their meetings were few: he rarely had enough money to travel to Paris; she came to America only once, for her lecture tour in 1934, and found him when he was traveling through Minnesota. Yet their corre-spondence reflected the mutual respect and appreciation which is evident in the selection that follows. Stein never failed in her praise of his work, declaring that "except Sherwood there was no one in America who could write a clear and passionate sentence."

In his introduction to her collection *Geography and Plays,* he wrote that "there is in America an impression of Miss Stein's personality, not at all true and rather foolishly romantic . . . of . . . a languid woman lying on a couch, smoking cigarettes, sipping absinthes per-haps and looking out upon the world with tired, disdain-ful eyes." In "Gertrude Stein's Kitchen" he does his best to dispel the myth and portray the woman he knew.

🌻 *Sherwood Anderson / from*

"Four American Impressions"

One who thinks a great deal about people and what
they are up to in the world comes inevitably in time to
relate them to experiences connected with his own life.
The round hard apples in this old orchard are the
breasts of my beloved. The curved round hill in the
distance is the body of my beloved, lying asleep. I cannot avoid practicing this trick of lifting people out of
the spots on which in actual life they stand and trans-
ferring them to what seems at the moment some more
fitting spot in the fanciful world.

And I get also a kind of aroma from people. They
are green healthy growing things or they have begun to
decay. There is something in this man, to whom I have
just talked, that has sent me away from him smiling and
in an odd way pleased with myself. Why has this other
man, although his words were kindly and his deeds apparently good, spread a cloud over my sky?

In my own boyhood in an Ohio town I went about
delivering newspapers at kitchen doors, and there were
certain houses to which I went—old brick houses with
immense old-fashioned kitchens—in which I loved to
linger. On Saturday mornings I sometimes managed to
collect a fragrant cooky at such a place but there was
something else that held me. Something got into my
mind connected with the great light kitchens and the
women working in them that came sharply back when,
last year, I went to visit an American woman, Miss
Gertrude Stein, in her own large room in the house at

71

27 rue de Fleurus in Paris. In the great kitchen of my fanciful world in which, ever since that morning, I have seen Miss Stein standing there is a most sweet and gracious aroma. Along the walls are many shining pots and pans, and there are innumerable jars of fruits, jellies and preserves. Something is going on in the great room, for Miss Stein is a worker in words with the same loving touch in her strong fingers that was characteristic of the women of the kitchens of the brick houses in the town of my boyhood. She is an American woman of the old sort, one who cares for the handmade goodies and who scorns the factory-made foods, and in her own great kitchen she is making something with her materials, something sweet to the tongue and fragrant to the nostrils.

That her materials are the words of our English speech and that we do not, most of us, know or care too much what she is up to does not greatly matter to me. The impression I wish now to give you of her is of one very intent and earnest in a matter most of us have forgotten. She is laying word against word, relating sound to sound, feeling for the taste, the smell, the rhythm of the individual word. She is attempting to do something for the writers of our English speech that may be better understood after a time, and she is not in a hurry.

And I have always that picture of the woman in the great kitchen of words, standing there by a table, clean, strong, with red cheeks and sturdy legs, always quietly and smilingly at work. If her smile has in it something of the mystery, to the male at least, of the Mona Lisa, I remember that the women in the kitchens on the wintry mornings wore often that same smile.

She is making new, strange and to my ears sweet combinations of words. As an American writer I admire her because she, in her person, represents something sweet and healthy in our American life, and because

I have a kind of undying faith that what she is up to in her word kitchen in Paris is of more importance to writers of English than the work of many of our more easily understood and more widely accepted word artists.

ERNEST HEMINGWAY

In 1922 Hemingway arrived in Paris armed with a letter of introduction from Sherwood Anderson to Gertrude Stein. "He is a delightful fellow and I like his talk," Stein soon wrote to Anderson. Years later, when their friendship had long since grown cold, she still remembered his "truly sensitive capacity for emotion . . . the stuff of the first stories." But her almost maternal admiration lasted only a short while. She saw that he was going "the way so many other Americans have gone before, the way they are still going. He became obsessed by sex and violent death."

Hemingway, at twenty-three, wavered between what Robert McAlmon called his "small-boy, tough-guy swagger" and what Sylvia Beach knew as his true vulnerability:

> Joyce remarked to me one day that he thought it was a mistake, Hemingway's thinking himself such a tough fellow and McAlmon trying to pass himself off as the sensitive type. It was the other way round, he thought.

When he was not at his ramshackle apartment on the crumbling rue Notre-Dame-des-Champs, or on an assignment for the *Toronto Star,* Hemingway would often be at Shakespeare and Company. He was not, Samuel Putnam noted, "a habitué of the cafes"; he was a disciplined writer, and if he sipped a cold beer at the

Closerie des Lilas, it was at the end of a day of serious work. But there was always time for his friendship with Sylvia Beach. He called himself her best customer, and he often came into the shop hand in hand with his son, nicknamed Bumby. "Hemingway was a widely educated young man," Miss Beach thought, ". . . and he had learned it all at first hand, not in universities." He confided to her about his youth in Illinois, his father's death, the necessity of his leaving school to earn a living for his family. The recollections were tinged with bitterness. In Sylvia Beach he found sympathy and genuine understanding. With her he could drop the defensive pose—what Stein called his "big Kansas-City boy brutality"—which he felt it necessary to assume with many others.

But for advice on writing he turned to Gertrude Stein, to whom he listened with "passionately interested" eyes. "Begin over again and concentrate," she told him, when his problems seemed insurmountable. And, she advised him, he must quit newspaper work. Newspaper writers, she thought, "have a false sense of time." They cannot consider the time in which they are writing, nor the time in which an event took place, but must always be conscious of the time the newspaper is coming out. Hemingway, she decided, never overcame this problem.

If she could not influence his sense of time, she did—though later he was reluctant to admit it—influence his style. Writing, he confessed in a letter to her, "used to be easy before I met you." In gratitude, he enthusiastically worked to help make her known, and succeeded in getting some of her work published in the *Transatlantic Review*.

His own writing brought to the surface the disillusionment that was carefully buried in Stein's work. She told him one day that his was a lost generation, and after an immediate reaction of hurt denial, he decided "that all generations were lost by something and always had been and always would be." Stein's offhand remark became the epigram for an age. But the excerpt from Ecclesiastes that Hemingway placed beside it as a preface to *The Sun Also Rises* more faithfully echoes Stein's own resignation to the pain of daily living. "After all," she wrote, "human beings have to live . . . so as not to know that time is passing, that is the whole business of living to go on so they will not know that time is passing, that is why they get drunk that is why they like to go to war. . . ." If hers was a lost generation, then the legendary Mother of Them All was as much a child of it as Hemingway. Yet she escaped the fate of so many of her contemporaries through conscious determination: ". . . our light is lit and the shutters are open, and perhaps everybody will find out, as the French know so well, that the winner loses, and everybody will be, too, like the French, that is, tremendously occupied with the business of daily living, and that will be enough."

🌿 *Ernest Hemingway / from* A Moveable Feast

When we came back to Paris it was clear and cold and lovely. The city had accommodated itself to winter, there was good wood for sale at the wood and coal place across our street, and there were braziers outside of many of the good cafés so that you could keep warm on the terraces. Our own apartment was warm and cheerful. We burned *boulets* which were molded, egg-shaped lumps of coal dust, on the wood fire, and on the streets the winter light was beautiful. Now you were accustomed to see the bare trees against the sky and you walked on the fresh-washed gravel paths through the Luxembourg Gardens in the clear sharp wind. The trees were sculpture without their leaves when you were reconciled to them, and the winter winds blew across the surfaces of the ponds and the fountains blew in the bright light. All the distances were short now since we had been in the mountains.

Because of the change in altitude I did not notice the grade of the hills except with pleasure, and the climb up to the top floor of the hotel where I worked, in a room that looked across all the roofs and chimneys of the high hill of the quarter, was a pleasure. The fireplace drew well in the room and it was warm and pleasant to work. I brought mandarines and roasted chestnuts to the room in paper packets and peeled and ate the small tangerine-like oranges and threw their skins and spat their seeds in the fire when I ate them and roasted chestnuts when I was hungry. I was always hungry with the walking and the cold and the working. Up in the room I had a bottle of kirsch that we had brought back from the mountains and I took a drink of kirsch when I would get toward the end of a story or toward the end of the day's work. When I was through working for the day I put away the notebook, or the paper, in the drawer of the table and put any mandarines that were left in my pocket. They would freeze if they were left in the room at night.

It was wonderful to walk down the long flights of stairs knowing that I'd had good luck working. I always worked until I had something done and I always stopped when I knew what was going to happen next. That way I could be sure of going on the next day. But sometimes when I was starting a new story and I could not get it going, I would sit in front of the fire and squeeze the peel of the little oranges into the edge of · the flame and watch the sputter of blue that they made. I would stand and look out over the roofs of Paris and think, "Do not worry. You have always written before and you will write now. All you have to do is write one true sentence. Write the truest sentence that you know." So finally I would write one true sentence, and then go on from there. It was easy then because there was always one true sentence that I knew or had seen or had heard someone say. If I started to write elaborately, or like someone introducing or presenting something, I found that I could cut that scrollwork or ornament out and throw it away and start with the first true simple declarative sentence I had written. Up in that room I decided that I would write one story about each thing that I knew about. I was trying to do this all the time I was writing, and it was good and severe discipline.

It was in that room too that I learned not to think about anything that I was writing from the time I stopped writing until I started again the next day. That way my subconscious would be working on it and at the same time I would be listening to other people and noticing everything, I hoped; learning, I hoped; and I would read so that I would not think about my work and make myself impotent to do it. Going down the stairs when I had worked well, and that needed luck as well as discipline, was a wonderful feeling and I was free then to walk anywhere in Paris.

If I walked down by different streets to the Jardin du Luxembourg in the afternoon I could walk through the gardens and then go to the Musée du Luxembourg where the great paintings were that have now mostly been transferred to the Louvre and the Jeu de Paume. I went there nearly every day for the Cézannes and to see the Manets and the Monets and the other Impressionists that I had first come to know about in the Art Institute at Chicago. I was learning something from the painting of Cézanne that made writing simple true sentences far from enough to make the stories have the dimensions that I was trying to put into them. I was learning very much from him but I was not articulate enough to explain it to anyone. Besides it was a secret. But if the light was gone in the Luxembourg I would walk up through the gardens and stop in at the studio apartment where Gertrude Stein lived at 27 rue de Fleurus.

My wife and I had called on Miss Stein, and she and the friend who lived with her had been very cordial and friendly and we had loved the big studio with the great paintings. It was like one of the best rooms in the finest museum except there was a big fireplace and it was warm and comfortable and they gave you good things to eat and tea and natural distilled liqueurs made from purple plums, yellow plums or wild raspberries. These were fragrant, colorless alcohols served from cut-glass carafes in small glasses and whether they were *quetsche, mirabelle* or *framboise* they all tasted like the fruits they came from, converted into a controlled fire on your tongue that warmed you and loosened it.

Miss Stein was very big but not tall and was heavily built like a peasant woman. She had beautiful eyes and a strong German-Jewish face that also could have been Friulano and she reminded me of a northern Italian peasant woman with her clothes, her mobile face and her lovely, thick, alive immigrant hair which she wore put up in the same way she had probably worn it in college. She talked all the time and at first it was about people and places.

Her companion had a very pleasant voice, was small, very dark, with her hair cut like Joan of Arc in the Boutet de Monvel illustrations and had a very hooked nose. She was working on a piece of needlepoint when we first met them and she worked on this and saw to the food and drink and talked to my wife. She made one conversation and listened to two and often interrupted the one she was not making. Afterwards she explained to me that she always talked to the wives. The wives, my wife and I felt, were tolerated. But we liked Miss Stein and her friend, although the friend was frightening. The paintings and the cakes and the *eau-de-vie* were truly wonderful. They seemed to like us too and treated us as though we were very good, well mannered and promising children and I felt that they forgave us for being in love and being married—time would fix that—and when my wife invited them to tea, they accepted.

When they came to our flat they seemed to like us even more; but perhaps that was because the place was so small and we were much closer together. Miss Stein sat on the bed that was on the floor and asked to see the stories I had written and she said that she liked them except one called "Up in Michigan."

"It's good," she said. "That's not the question at all. But it is *inaccrochable*. That means it is like a picture that a painter paints and then he cannot hang it when he has a show and nobody will buy it because they cannot hang it either."

"But what if it is not dirty but it is only that you are trying to use words that people would actually use? That are the only words that can make the story come true and that you must use them? You have to use them."

"But you don't get the point at all," she said. "You mustn't write anything that is *inaccrochable*. There is no point in it. It's wrong and it's silly."

She herself wanted to be published in the *Atlantic Monthly*, she told me, and she would be. She told me that I was not a good enough writer to be published there or in the *Saturday Evening Post* but that I might be some new sort of writer in my own way but the first thing to remember was not to write stories that were *inaccrochable*. I did not argue about this nor try to explain again what I was trying to do about conversation. That was my own business and it was much more interesting to listen. That afternoon she told us, too, how to buy pictures.

"You can either buy clothes or buy pictures," she said. "It's that simple. No one who is not very rich can do both. Pay no attention to your clothes and no attention at all to the mode, and buy your clothes for comfort and durability, and you will have the clothes money to buy pictures."

"But even if I never bought any more clothing ever," I said, "I wouldn't have enough money to buy the Picassos that I want."

"No. He's out of your range. You have to buy the people of your own age—of your own military service group. You'll know them. You'll meet them around the quarter. There are always good new serious painters. But it's not you buying clothes so much. It's your wife always. It's women's clothes that are expensive."

I saw my wife trying not to look at the strange, steerage clothes that Miss Stein wore and she was successful. When they left we were still popular, I thought, and we were asked to come again to 27 rue de Fleurus.

It was later on that I was asked to come to the studio any time after five in the winter time. I had met Miss Stein in the Luxembourg. I cannot remember whether she was walking her dog or not, nor whether she had a dog then. I know that I was walking myself, since we could not afford a dog nor even a cat then, and the only cats I knew were in the cafés or small restaurants or the great cats that I admired in concierges' windows. Later I often met Miss Stein with her dog in the Luxembourg Gardens; but I think this time was before she had one.

But I accepted her invitation, dog or no dog, and had taken to stopping in at the studio, and she always gave me the natural *eau-de-vie,* insisting on my refilling my glass, and I looked at the pictures and we talked. The pictures were exciting and the talk was very good. She talked, mostly, and she told me about modern pictures and about painters—more about them as people than as painters—and she talked about her work. She showed me the many volumes of manuscript that she had written and that her companion typed each day. Writing every day made her happy, but as I got to know her better I found that for her to keep happy it was necessary that this steady daily output, which varied with her energy, be published and that she receive recognition.

This had not become an acute situation when I first knew her, since she had published three stories that were intelligible to anyone. One of these stories, "Melanctha," was very good and good samples of her experimental writing had been published in book form and had been well praised by critics who had met her or known her. She had such a personality that when she wished to win anyone over to her side she would not be resisted, and critics who met her and saw her pictures took on trust writing of hers that they could not understand because of their enthusiasm for her as a person, and because of their confidence in her judgment. She had also discovered many truths about rhythms and the uses of words in repetition that were valid and valuable and she talked well about them.

But she disliked the drudgery of revision and the obligation to make her writing intelligible, although she needed to have publication and official acceptance, especially for the unbelievably long book called *The Making of Americans*.

This book began magnificently, went on very well for a long way with great stretches of great brilliance and then went on endlessly in repetitions that a more conscientious and less lazy writer would have put in the waste basket. I came to know it very well as I got—forced, perhaps would be the word—Ford Madox Ford to publish it in the *Transatlantic Review* serially, knowing that it would outrun the life of the review. For publication in the review I had to read all of Miss Stein's proof for her as this was a work which gave her no happiness.

On this cold afternoon when I had come past the concierge's lodge and the cold courtyard to the warmth of the studio, all that was years ahead. On this day Miss Stein was instructing me about sex. By that time we liked each other very much and I had already learned that everything I did not understand probably had something to it. Miss Stein thought that I was too uneducated about sex and I must admit that I had certain prejudices against homosexuality since I knew its more primitive aspects. I knew it was why you carried a knife and would use it when you were in the company of tramps when you were a boy in the days when wolves was not a slang term for men obsessed by the pursuit of women.

I knew many *inaccrochable* terms and phrases from Kansas City days and the mores of different parts of that city, Chicago and the lake boats. Under questioning I tried to tell Miss Stein that when you were a boy and moved in the company of men, you have to be prepared to kill a man, know how to do it and really know that you would do it in order not to be interfered with. That term was *accrochable*. If you knew you would kill, other people sensed it very quickly and you were let alone; but there were certain situations you could not allow yourself to be forced into or trapped into. I could have expressed myself more vividly by using an *inaccrochable* phrase that wolves used on the lake boats, "Oh gash may be fine but one eye for mine." But I was always careful of my language with Miss Stein even when true phrases might have clarified or better expressed a prejudice.

"Yes, yes, Hemingway," she said. "But you were living in a milieu of criminals and perverts."

I did not want to argue that, although I thought that I had lived in a world as it was and there were all kinds of people in it and I tried to understand them, although some of them I could not like and some I still hated.

"But what about the old man with beautiful manners and a great name who came to the hospital in Italy and brought me a bottle of Marsala or Campari and behaved perfectly, and then one day I would have to tell the nurse never to let that man into the room again?" I asked.

"Those people are sick and cannot help themselves and you should pity them."

"Should I pity so and so?" I asked. I gave his name but he delights so in giving it himself that I feel there is no need to give it for him.

"No. He's vicious. He's a corrupter and he's truly vicious."

"But he's supposed to be a good writer."

"He's not," she said. "He's just a showman and he corrupts for the pleasure of corruption and he leads people into other vicious practices as well. Drugs, for example."

"And in Milan the man I'm to pity was not trying to corrupt me?"

"Don't be silly. How could he hope to corrupt you? Do you corrupt a boy like you, who drinks alcohol, with a bottle of Marsala? No, he was a pitiful old man who could not help what he was doing. He was sick and he could not help it and you should pity him."

"I did at the time," I said. "But I was disappointed because he had such beautiful manners."

I took another sip of the *eau-de-vie* and pitied the old man and looked at Picasso's nude of the girl with the basket of flowers. I had not started the conversation and thought it had become a little dangerous. There were almost never any pauses in a conversation with Miss Stein, but we had paused and there was something she wanted to tell me and I filled my glass.

"You know nothing about any of this really, Hemingway," she said. "You've met known criminals and sick people and vicious people. The main thing is that the act male homosexuals commit is ugly and repugnant and afterwards they are disgusted with themselves. They drink and take drugs, to palliate this, but they are disgusted with the act and they are always changing partners and cannot be really happy."

"I see."

"In women it is the opposite. They do nothing that they are disgusted by and nothing that is repulsive and afterwards they are happy and they can lead happy lives together."

"I see," I said. "But what about so and so?"

"She's vicious," Miss Stein said. "She's truly vicious, so she can never be happy except with new people. She corrupts people."

"I understand."

"You're sure you understand?"

There were so many things to understand in those days and I was glad when we talked about something else. The park was closed so I had to walk down along it to the rue de Vaugirard and around the lower end of the park. It was sad when the park was closed and locked and I was sad walking around it instead of through it and in a hurry to get home to the rue Cardinal Lemoine. The day had started out so brightly too. I would have to work hard tomorrow. Work could cure almost anything, I believed then, and I believe now. Then all I had to be cured of, I decided Miss Stein felt, was youth and loving my wife. I was not at all sad when I got home to the rue Cardinal Lemoine and told my newly acquired knowledge to my wife. In the night we were happy with our own knowledge we already had and other new knowledge we had acquired in the mountains.

MAN RAY

Man Ray, one of the few Americans associated with early Dadaism, was born to Russian-Jewish parents in 1890 and changed his name to monosyllables when he was a young artist studying in Manhattan.

Like most artists of his time, he left home early, but instead of going directly to Paris, he moved to an art colony in Ridgefield, New Jersey, where he began a lifelong friendship with Marcel Duchamp. He did not make his way to Paris until Bastille Day, 1921.

Man Ray soon became the official portraitist for the writers and artists living in Paris, and his photographs covered the walls of Shakespeare and Company. "To be 'done' by Man Ray and Berenice Abbott [then his assistant] meant you were rated as somebody," Sylvia Beach noted. But portraits were not Man Ray's prime interest. His experiments in photography and other media occupied more of his creative energy. In 1922 he accidentally discovered that objects left on sensitized photographic paper would produce a distorted silhouette. The results, which he dubbed rayographs, were much admired by Tristan Tzara and his fellow Dadaists.

Part of Man Ray's reputation derived from his intimate association with the notorious Parisian model Kiki, often his subject; part from his involvement with Dadaism and later, after Dadaism was proclaimed dead, with Surrealism. He was the creator of two of the principal Surrealist films—*Emak Bahia* and *The Star-fish*—which stand with the works of Buñuel and Dali as cinematic innovations.

Best known as a photographer, Man Ray neverthe-less felt ambivalent in his allegiance to any one medium. In a 1938 essay, "Photography as Consolation," he ad-vises his fellow photographers to "smile . . . but if your hand trembles too much, leave your camera there and take up a brush." Painting, he felt, "was an adventure in which some unknown force might suddenly change the whole aspect of things. The result could be as much a surprise to myself as to a spectator."

His technique for portraiture interested Gertrude Stein. "He said move all you like, your eyes, your head, it is to be a pose but it is to have in it all the qualities of a snap shot." She did as he directed, sitting through very long poses, and found the results "extraordinarily interesting."

🌿 *Man Ray / from* Self Portrait

My first visit to Gertrude Stein in the rue de Fleurus, shortly after my arrival in France, caused me mixed sensations. Crossing the courtyard, I rang a bell; the door was opened by a small dark woman with long earrings, looking like a gypsy. Inside, I was greeted with a broad smile by Gertrude Stein, massive, in a woolen dress and woolen socks with comfortable sandals, which emphasized her bulk. I had brought my camera; it was understood that I was to make some pictures of her in her interior. Miss Stein introduced me to her friend Alice Toklas, whom I had taken for her maid, although, in her print dress trimmed with white lace, she was too carefully groomed. Miss Stein, too, wore a flowered blouse fastened at the neck with a scarf held by a Victorian brooch. Both sat down in chintz-covered armchairs blending with their dresses, while I set up my camera. The room was filled with massive waxed Italian and Spanish furniture on which stood knicknacks in porcelain, with here and there a small vase containing posies, all of which was discreetly set off by a neutral wainscoting. At one end of the room, between two small windows, hung a large black cross. But above, all around the room were paintings by Cézanne, Matisse, Braque, and Picasso on a light water-stained wall. At first glance it was difficult to reconcile the effect of these with the more traditional setting below. The intention, no doubt, was to prove that the two different elements could cohabit. If anything, what were considered revolutionary paintings seemed to blend with the older

89

stuff. This was emphasized by the Cézannes and Barques which hung above the ornamental fireplace and had acquired some of its soot. I wished these had kept their original brilliance for my photography.

In another corner hung the portrait of Gertrude Stein by Picasso, a good likeness—I had her sit alongside it for a double portrait. Like many of his more conventional works, it looked unfinished but the hands were beautifully painted. I have no objection to unfinished works, in fact I have an aversion to paintings in which nothing is left to speculation. Certainly, my photographs left nothing to the imagination, that is, my straight photography; I was already trying to overcome this deficiency in my freer work which I pursued on the side. This aroused the interest of a few who closely followed all the newer trends in expression; in general it left others indifferent, those who had no imagination. I must include among these most of my sitters, intent on getting an important-looking image of themselves.

My portraits of Gertrude Stein were the first to appear in print, to give her small circle of readers at the time an idea of how she looked. Perhaps I was impressed by the staidness of her personality but it never occurred to me to try any fantasy or acrobatics with her physiognomy. She might have welcomed the notoriety, as in her writing; and she might have thought more of me as a creative artist. Besides the classics on her walls, she took an interest now and then in some striving young painter—tried to help him, but soon dropped him so that generally he passed into oblivion. It reminds me of a famous gourmet in France who was approached by a manufacturer of margarine to write a phrase extolling the merits of his product. The gourmet wrote: Nothing can replace butter! Gertrude Stein was mature and hardened; nothing that came after her first attachments could equal them. This attitude was carried to the extreme regarding other writers—they were all

condemned: Hemingway, Joyce, the Dadaists, the Surrealists, with herself as the pioneer. Her bitterness really
showed up when the others got universal attention before she did. In her own circle she always held the floor;
if anyone tried to usurp it, that person was shortly called
to order. One day at a small gathering, she and two of
us engaged in conversation at one end of the room; in
an opposite corner Alice and a woman carried on a lively dialogue. Gertrude stopped short, turned her head in
their direction and shouted belligerently for them to
lower their voices. It was more than effective—there
was a dead silence.

I visited often during the next ten years, she came to
my studio for other sittings, and invited me to lunch—
Alice's cooking was famous. One of the last sittings,
with her hair cropped after an illness, pleased her
especially. She looked rather mannish, except for her
flowered blouse and the brooch she always wore. In
exchange for some prints she did a portrait of me in
prose.

By now she had publishers and a public. Requiring
photographs for her publicity she ordered a dozen
prints which I sent with a modest bill. Soon I received
a short note saying that we were all struggling artists,
that it was I who had invited her to sit for me, and not
she who had solicited me, in short, not to be silly. I did
not answer, thinking that she felt I was indebted to her
—in any case, I had told her in a previous note, when
my pictures of her were reproduced in magazines, that
I would do what I could to help her. But I, too, was
getting known and had the reputation of being a very
expensive photographer, perhaps because I sent out bills
more often, when I thought sitters could pay something.
It wasn't so much the money I was after—there were
plenty of clients who never quibbled and paid enough
to make up for those who did not, but I felt more and
more that I was being kept from more creative work;

I expected a sacrifice from those who were concerned with themselves alone. The flattery and glory that came from portraiture that was often drudgery left me cold. Sometimes, when a prospective client found my price high, I replied ironically that if he or she would like a portrait of myself, it would cost nothing.

Gertrude Stein lived well during her long stay in Paris, whether she already had money from her family, or occasionally sold a painting from her collection— she certainly did not make enough from her writings. When success finally came, she managed her contracts for books and lectures very efficiently—whereas I had started with nothing but my own efforts. I granted that she had made an important contribution to contemporary literature, had been especially helpful to starving European artists, but had profited all she could from her initiative. On one occasion when a collector wished to buy a painting from her, but observed that she was asking more than a work of similiar importance brought in the galleries, she replied, Ah, yes, but the latter was not from the Gertrude Stein collection.

JO DAVIDSON

Jo Davidson completed his seated figure of Gertrude Stein in 1923. The nearly life-size sculpture captures Miss Stein's presence, as the critic Edmund Wilson recognized:

> We picture her as the great pyramidal Buddha of Jo Davidson's statue of her, eternally and placidly ruminating the gradual developments of the processes of being, registering the vibrations of a psychological country like some august human seismograph whose charts we haven't the training to read.

Born in 1883, Davidson spent his childhood partly in his home on the Lower East Side of New York and partly in "a wooden shack away out in the country at 109th Street and Riverside Drive," where he scampered barefoot through patches of wild berries. He was introduced to art through drawing classes at the Educational Alliance. His sister, recognizing his talent, arranged for the payment of tuition at the Art Students League, where Davidson became an assistant to an artist working in burned leather. He later attended the Yale Art School, where he first experienced the thrill of discovering clay.

> One day, wandering through the building, I found myself in a room full of plaster casts and modeling

stands—and not a soul in it. I found the clay bin, put my hand in it, and touched the beginning of my life.

His almost mystical reaction to the medium led to increasing dissatisfaction with the instruction he was getting at Yale. In 1907 he arrived in Paris to join the struggling, starving community of young artists. He continued sculpting, largely unknown, until he sold his first piece to Mrs. Harry Payne Whitney and through her gained a reputation among wealthy buyers in New York and Paris.

Best known for his lifelike busts and heads, Davidson had for subjects such diverse individuals as Woodrow Wilson, James Joyce, George Bernard Shaw, Gandhi, Einstein, and Charlie Chaplin.

❧ *Jo Davidson* / *from* Between Sittings

1923 was a very busy year. I did the portrait of Gertrude Stein that year.

To do a head of Gertrude was not enough—there was so much more to her than that. So I did a seated figure of her—a sort of modern Buddha.

I had known her since my first trip to France. She and her brother Leo had two adjoining studios. Doors had been cut through, connecting the two studios; and every Saturday afternoon, the studios were jammed with visitors of various nationalities, either gaping, in earnest discussions, or laughing at the Matisses and the Picassos. Gertrude would stand with her back to the fireplace, her hands clasped behind her back, watching the crowd like a Cambodian caryatid, wearing a smile of patience, looking as if she knew something that nobody else did.

In the other studio, Leo, tall and lean, with a red beard, would talk earnestly about aesthetics to anyone who was prepared to listen. In the excitement of his conversation, he generally twisted a button of his listener's waistcoat until it became a straightjacket. One could not get a word in edgewise. All one could do was to wait patiently for him to let go of the button and then make an escape.

Years later I was walking along Fifth Avenue in New York when I ran into Leo Stein. He was no longer bearded, and was wearing a conspicuous hearing-aid. He greeted me effusively: "Remember when I used to talk and talk and never would listen. Now I want to hear and can't."

Yvonne* and I became great friends of Gertrude Stein and Alice Toklas. Gertrude's was a very rich personality. Her wit and her laughter were contagious. She loved good food and served it. While I was doing her portrait, she would come around to my studio with a manuscript and read it aloud. The extraordinary part of it was that, as she read, I never felt any sense of mystification. "A rose is a rose is a rose," took on a different meaning with each inflection. When she read aloud, I got the humor of it. We both laughed, and her laughter was something to hear. There was an eternal quality about her—she somehow symbolized wisdom.

Gertrude did a portrait of me in prose. When she read it aloud, I thought it was wonderful. It was published in *Vanity Fair* with my portrait of her. But when I tried to read it out loud to some friends, or for that matter to myself, it didn't make much sense.

*Davidson's wife.

Pablo Picasso, *Gertrude Stein* (1906)
The Metropolitan Museum of Art,
Bequest of Gertrude Stein, 1946

Pablo Picasso, *Homage To Gertrude* (1909)
Private Collection, New York

Alvin Langdon Coburn, *Portrait of Gertrude Stein* (1913)
Collection, International Museum of Photography at
George Eastman House, Rochester

Jacques Lipchitz, *Gertrude Stein* (1920)
Collection, The Museum of Modern Art, New York

Jo Davidson, *Gertrude Stein* (1920)
Collection, Whitney Museum of American Art, New York

Pavel Tchelitchew, *Portrait of Gertrude Stein* (c. 1930)
Courtesy of The Art Institute of Chicago

Francis Rose, *Gertrude Stein* (1930-1935)
Private Collection

Francis Picabia, *Gertrude Stein* (early 1930's)
Private Collection

Carl Van Vechten, *Gertrude Stein* (1934)
Courtesy of the Estate of Carl Van Vechten

ALVIN LANGDON COBURN

Alvin Langdon Coburn began his "adventure in photography" with a Kodak box camera given to him as a child by his uncles. His first photograph was of his neighbor's playful dog. By the time he was sixteen he had amassed an impressive portfolio, and his distant cousin, the wealthy photographer and publisher F. Holland Day, invited him to take part in an exhibition day he was planning in London.

The trip abroad opened a new world to Coburn. From London he traveled with his cousin and his mother to Paris, where, he later wrote, "you could get coffee with whipped cream in settings which were period pieces of life in a truly artistic background." But though he was enamored of Europe, he returned home to Boston and then moved to New York, where he opened a studio on Fifth Avenue. He thought himself no less than an artist, although photography, in 1902, "was hardly considered as an art . . . It had its battle to fight and win, but it was to achieve victory by virtue of its own merits—by the unique subtlety of its tonal range and its capacity to explore and exploit the infinite gradations of luminosity, rather than by imitating the technique of the draughtsman."*

*Alvin Langdon Coburn, Photographer, An Autobiography edited by Helmut and Alison Gernsheim (N.Y. Praeger, 1966)

He found portraiture a sensitive means of expression, and his subjects include the greatest men of his time. Bernard Shaw was the first literary lion he captured. G. K. Chesterton, Mark Twain, Yeats, H. G. Wells, Matisse, Pound, and Stravinsky followed.

In 1913 he again visited Paris, this time accompanied by his wife of a few months. It was, he recalled, "a continuation of our honeymoon." In April he wrote to Gertrude Stein for permission to see her "splendid collection of paintings by Matisse" and was granted a visit to the rue de Fleurus. He became the first photographer to render her portrait "as a celebrity" and she admitted being "nicely gratified." He felt that she was a true pioneer in art, using words "for their tonal value" and exploring "fresh and spontaneous modes of approach." Realizing her respect for Henry James, Coburn tried— unsuccessfully—to arrange a meeting between the two writers. He did manage, however, to publicize her writing in England, the country he had adopted as his home.

The experiments in art and literature that marked the years before World War I did not fail to influence Coburn. In 1916 he devised an instrument composed of three mirrors fastened together in the form of a triangle, which acted as a prism to split images into kaleidoscopic segments. He called his invention a "Vortoscope," adapting its name from the "Vorticist" movement—an outgrowth of Futurism and Cubism—begun by Ezra Pound and Wyndham Lewis in 1914. The abstract photographs that resulted from this technique are characterized by the same gentle, muted tones and poetic mood of his portraits.

Having spent most of his adult life in England, Coburn followed the example of Henry James and became a British subject in 1932. He spent the remainder of his life in North Wales, in his home Awen, Welsh for Inspiration.

JACQUES LIPCHITZ

His father, a building contractor, wanted him to become an architect; but with his mother's help Chaim Jacob Lipchitz left Lithuania for Paris in 1909 to study sculpture at the Ecole des Beaux-Arts. Fifteen years later, when he became a French citizen, Jacques Lipchitz ranked with Modigliani, Picasso, and Juan Gris in the forefront of modern art.

He was excitedly involved in Cubist sculpture at the time he met Gertrude Stein in 1915. Cubism, he felt, was "an emancipation from Mother Nature . . . a moment when humanity had come out of the womb of nature to the beginning of a new independence." But although Stein's sympathies were clearly with similar experiments by such artists as Picasso and Braque, she had always preferred painting to sculpture and even the charming young Lipchitz could not succeed in interesting her in collecting his work. She was, however, attracted to him because he was "an excellent gossip," and when she sat for him in 1920 he was able to provide "several missing parts of many stories," much to her delight.

For Lipchitz, portraiture was a pleasure as well as a source of income (although Stein failed to buy the completed work). "All my life, with a few intervals, I have done portraits," he recalled. "I love to do them, and no matter what else I am working on I find them an excellent discipline and even relaxation." In portraying Stein he was especially concerned about her eyes. In the first model, now at the Musée National de l'Art Moderne in Paris, the eyes were rendered naturalistically. But this did not achieve a sufficient impression of the "shadowed introspection" that he felt characterized his subject; finally Lipchitz deeply hollowed out the eyes, and was satisfied with the effect.

Eighteen years later he again met Gertrude Stein, and was struck by her loss of weight and her changed presence. "The massive, self-confident Buddha has become a tired and rather tragic old woman." She sat for him once more while he tried to capture her as "a shriveled old rabbi, with a little rabbi's cap on her head." Two sketches resulted, vastly different from the stark yet graceful roundness of the 1920 work.

The 1938 meeting was their last, for Lipchitz fled from Paris in 1940, immediately before Hitler's occupation, carrying with him a vial of poison he had obtained from a doctor friend: "I felt that I would rather die than fall into Hitler's hands." From Toulouse, where he was able to work for a while, he came to America. After his New York studio was destroyed by fire in 1952, he moved to Hastings-on-Hudson, and then, ten years later, returned to Europe—this time to Italy. There, until his death in 1973, he worked tirelessly. "I am still, like my father, putting one brick after another in the building of a house, attempting to make a final statement. I would like to be able to make this at the end of my life, or, as my father always said, 'to come to the roof.' "

PAVEL TCHELITCHEW

Like many Russian aristocrats, the family of Pavel Tchelitchew fled from its home during the Bolshevik Revolution. In 1918 Tchelitchew found himself in Kiev, where he studied drawing at the Kiev Academy. His flight continued, taking him to Turkey, to Berlin, and then to Paris in 1923. Much of his work was as a scenic designer for theater and ballet, including sets for Diaghilev's startling new company. His painting suggests inspiration from Picasso's ascetic Harlequins, which Tchelitchew stretched and distorted even further. Throughout his work, in the pained figures, shattered faces, and somber tones, there is evidence of his own suffering and torments. "Strindberg was said to have been possessed by a dark demon," Harold Acton commented, "but [Tchelitchew] must have been possessed by several."

The atmosphere in his Rue Jacques Mawas studio was fittingly macabre. There, Acton observed, the artist would spend his days moping in the company of his "stolid Russian sister and a Frenchified American friend who sat thumping the piano in his dressing gown." When he was able to paint, he devoted much of his creative energy to experimentation. "Though [Tchelitchew] pretended to have a horror of fashion," Acton again noted, "he could not help courting it." And fellow artist Francis Rose concurred, adding, "He was always searching and twisting in different directions, as if he were afraid of dropping behind the times." For a time he painted with a mixture of coffee grounds, sand, and gouache.

Although Gertrude Stein was pleased with his portrait of her, Acton felt an intense dislike for the bald, elongated head and clotted forehead that Tchelitchew painted as his likeness. Like the portrait of Dorian Gray, it was, Acton feared, what he might become.

If Acton's response was less than enthusiastic, it was more than compensated by the support of Edith Sitwell. Gertrude Stein introduced the painter to the poet and she quickly became one of his favorite subjects. Dame Edith dedicated two poems to him, sat for six portraits and a sculpture in wax on wire, and described him as "that tragic, haunted, and noble artist—one of the most generous human beings I have even known."

Although Tchelitchew was successful as an artist in France, he was never able to consider it his home. He felt intensely foreign, he admitted in a letter to Gertrude Stein. He considered himself "a Russian Negro among the French."

Before World War II, Tchelitchew left Paris and immigrated to the United States. In his New York studio he began a satirical surrealistic painting, *Phenomena,* which showed, among other things, Gertrude Stein squatting on a heap of broken canvas. Tchelitchew died in 1957.

FRANCIS PICABIA

Although he was acknowledged by André Breton as one of the pillars of Surrealism, Francis Picabia preferred to be aligned with no movement. "One must be a nomad, pass through ideas as one passes through countries and cities."

Born in Paris of Cuban parents, he never lost his Latin temper nor his reputation for inventiveness and independence. As a "nomad" in art, he passed through Impressionism and Cubism until, in 1918, he joined the exploding Dadaist group in Zurich. "What I like is to invent," he wrote later, "to imagine, to make myself a new man every moment, then forget him, forget everything." His innovations sometimes took the form of "object portraits": Alfred Stieglitz as a camera, for example; or the "American Girl" as a spark plug. "Those who do not understand will never understand and those who understand because they have to understand have no need of me," he wrote, defending himself in prose worthy of Stein.

His friendship with Gertrude Stein had a cool beginning; she was annoyed by "his incessantness" and what she called "the vulgarity of his delayed adolescence." But gradually his drawing and painting began to interest her, and she dubbed him "the Leonardo da Vinci of the movement."

Picabia has conceived and is struggling with the problem that a line should have the vibration of a musical sound and that this vibration should be the result of conceiving the human form and the human face in so tenuous a fashion that it would induce such vibration in the line forming it.

She found his views on painting congenial with her own, and he in turn took comfort in her approval. Their conversations about painting, he wrote to her, "confirmed in me the certitude that my experiments are working out."

As a token of his friendship he gave her a tiny Mexican chihuahua which Stein named Byron because he was to be mated with either his sister or his mother. When the dog suddenly died of typhus, Picabia replaced him with another, Pépé.

Picabia was a frequent guest at Bilignin, where he and Stein discussed the past and future of art and the peculiar responsibility of a genius. There are, Picabia explained, "men with antennas," able to feel and express the unsuspected in their environment. He professed to be influenced by no one—not by his grandfather, one of the inventors of photography, with whom he spent much of his youth; not even by Cézanne. He spoke so vehemently against the Master of Aix that Stein was at first shocked. Finally convinced, she admitted, "Everybody of that period was influenced by Cézanne but he says he was not and was not." He was an individual, and though she never went so far as to place him in her tiny elite of geniuses, his gifts impressed her. By 1936 he had won her over completely. "I am not interested in anybody painting," she wrote in *Everybody's Autobiography*. "Except Picabia."

PABLO PICASSO

For Gertrude Stein, genius was so rare a quality that it was possessed by only two living artists: herself and Pablo Picasso. Although Picasso modestly defined genius as "personality with a penny's worth of talent," he nevertheless acknowledged his uniqueness. "When I was a child," he recalled, "my mother said to me, 'If you become a soldier you'll be a general. If you become a monk you'll end up as the Pope.' Instead, I became a painter and wound up as Picasso."

It was Leo Stein who discovered Picasso's work at the gallery of Clovis Sagot, the impish art dealer who assured him that the paintings by this unknown Spaniard were "the real thing." He bought one—a mountebank with wife, child, and an ape—and returned to the gallery later with his sister. Leo wanted to purchase the *Young Girl with a Basket,* which Picasso had completed that spring, but Gertrude immediately hated the picture, especially the feet, and refused. Leo finally bought it over Gertrude's protest; a short time afterward he was taken to meet the artist, whom he visited amid the chaos and debris of the rue Ravignan studio, and invited him to the rue de Fleurus.

Gertrude Stein's response to Picasso was a striking reversal of her reaction to his work. He was "small, quick moving but not restless, his eyes having a strange faculty of opening wide and drinking in what he wished to see. He had the isolation and movement of the head of a bull-fighter at the head of their procession." She knew immediately that this odd young man, like her, was in the process of creating the twentieth century.

Picasso and his mistress Fernande Olivier were frequent guests at the Steins' dinners and Saturday evenings. In 1906, although he had not used a model for some eight years, Picasso asked Gertrude Stein to sit for a portrait. There followed some eighty visits to the artist's studio. On her walks from Montparnasse on the Left Bank to the hills of Montmartre across the Seine, Miss Stein worked out many of the ideas for "Melanctha," one of the stories in *Three Lives,* and thought, too, about the literary problems with which she was then struggling. Some of these she discussed with Picasso. "I was a little obsessed by words of equal value," she recalled in an interview shortly before her death, "and he and I used to talk this thing over endlessly. At this time he had just begun cubism."

"One had to break to make one's revolution and start at zero," Picasso felt. Gertrude Stein, agreeing, saw her task to be "not imitation either of sounds or colors or emotions" but "an intellectual recreation."

For Picasso, one of the first expressions of his revolution was *Les demoiselles d'Avignon* (1907); for Gertrude Stein, the experiments resulted in *Tender Buttons,* a book that she later admitted contained "as much failure as success." It was an effort to begin with an object and then, as Picasso said, "remove all traces of reality. There's no danger . . . because the idea of the object will have left an indelible mark."

The settings for their talks shifted back to the rue de Fleurus when Picasso abruptly ended the sittings, leaving the portrait incomplete. Yet years later, when the masklike face was painted in, it met with Gertrude Stein's approval. "It is the only reproduction of me which is always I, for me," she wrote.

For Picasso, portraiture made special demands upon an artist. "There are so many realities that in trying to encompass them all one ends in darkness. That is why, when one paints a portrait, one must stop somewhere, in a sort of caricature. Otherwise there would be nothing left at the end."

The portrait meant as much to him as it did to its owner, and when it was about to be shipped to the Metropolitan Museum of Art after Miss Stein's death, Picasso came to Alice Toklas' apartment to take a last look at it, bowed his head, and recited a prayer for the dead.

The legend that is Gertrude Stein lives, as Picasso knew it would, in his portrait. And the extraordinary temperament that was Picasso fills the pages of Stein's autobiographies. She knew he was more than an artist, for he lived his art in the way Cézanne had done, and his works, for her, had "meaning, a charming meaning, a solid meaning, a struggling meaning, a clear meaning." As Leo Stein put it: "Matisse said once that Cézanne is the 'father of us all,' but he did not reckon with the phoenix Picasso, who had no father."

EDITH SITWELL

When she was a young girl, Edith Sitwell was asked by one of her mother's friends that familiar question, "What are you going to be when you are grown up, little E?" To this the child unflinchingly replied, "A genius." The anecdote, reminiscent of Stein's own early realization of her individuality, gives a clue to the spiritual kinship that formed the basis of their friendship.

Dame Edith and Miss Stein were of markedly different appearance. Whereas Dame Edith remembered Gertrude Stein as looking like an Easter Island idol, Alice Toklas, looking back on the writers' first meeting, wrote:

> Miss Sitwell was a great surprise to us for she looked like nobody under the sun, very tall, rather the height of a grenadier, with marked features and the most beautiful nose any woman had.

She affected all who knew her with what Harold Acton called "a stellar radiance," and, he added, as she aged she seemed to grow more splendid. "The tall pale figure with flat hair from the Unicorn Tapestry . . . resembled Queen Elizabeth I, very regal and commanding, though 'always a little outside life.' "

Although Edith Sitwell's aristocratic elegance contrasted with Gertrude Stein's earthy presence, their literary experiments, stemming from a similar quest, resulted in mutual sympathy and understanding. Both, defending their creations, express parallel views.

Ordinary language and conventional usage were insufficient, Edith Sitwell explained, "to pierce down to the essence of the thing seen," to produce "its quintessential color (sharper, brighter than that seen by an eye grown stale)." Miss Stein agreed. "Poetry is concerned with using with abusing, with losing with wanting with denying with avoiding with adoring with replacing the noun . . ."

Sharing the same craft, the two became friends immediately on meeting and Dame Edith succeeded in persuading Gertrude Stein to come to Oxford and Cambridge to lecture in the spring of 1926. The lecture was followed by a reading of Stein's short pieces, "Preciosilla," "A Saint in Seven," "Sitwell Edith Sitwell," and "Jean Cocteau." The experience of lecturing proved to be less ominous than Miss Stein had feared and the English lectures became a prelude for the major speaking tour she undertook in America a few years later.

Edith Sitwell, regal, splendid, ethereal, died in London in 1964, leaving numerous collections of her sonorous, percussive verse, and a memoir which recalls Gertrude Stein with affection.

🌹 Edith Sitwell / from Taken Care Of

The two people whom I remember with pleasure . . . are Gertrude Stein and the painter Pavel Tchelitchew, to whom she introduced me. Gertrude was verbally very interesting, the more so as she invariably got everybody wrong. She looked rather like an Easter Island idol, was immensely good-humoured, and had a remarkable ability to work in the midst of any amount of noise. She had been known to sit in a garage while her motor was being repaired, writing with complete concentration. But she did not suffer fools gladly. Her salon, for which she was famous, was divided. Gertrude talked to the husbands, it was the job of Alice B. Toklas to entertain the wives and the less interesting of the guests. Sometimes it became apparent to the guests that they had been divided thus, and repeated attempts were made on their part to do something about it. Miss Toklas, however, remained firm.

I was, I am glad to say, always put next to Gertrude! It was at my invitation that she came to England later on to lecture in this country.

Her work is an illustration of the success and also of the dangers of revolution. She is the last writer in the world whom any other writer should take as a model; but her work, for the most part, is very valuable because of its revivifying qualities, and it contains, to my mind, considerable beauty.

"These artists," said Roger Fry in his catalogue to the second Post-Impressionist Exhibition, "do not seek to imitate life, but to find an equivalent for life. . . . In fact they aim not at illusion but at reality. The logical extreme of such a method would undoubtedly be the attempt to give up all resemblance to natural form, and to create a purely abstract language of form. . . ."

This seems applicable to Miss Stein, with her extremely strong visual sense, strengthened, no doubt, by her friendship with the most important painters of her day.

She said to me, in one of our conversations, "The difference between Picasso and inferior painters is that inferior painters put in all the leaves on a tree, with the result that you see neither tree nor leaves. Picasso paints one leaf upon a tree, and you see the life of the tree."

She threw a word into the air, and when it returned to the ground it bore within it the original meaning it bore before custom and misuse had blurred it.

"If we look at an isolated printed word," said William James in *Principles of Psychology*, "and repeat it long enough, it ends by assuming an entirely unnatural aspect . . . its body is indeed there, but its soul is fled. It is reduced, by this new way of attending to it, to its sensational nudity. We never before attended to it in this way, but habitually got it clad with its meaning the moment we caught sight of it, and rapidly passed from it to the other words of the phrase. We apprehended it, in short, with a cloud of associates, and thus perceiving it, we felt it quite otherwise than as we feel it now, divested and alone."

This, I think, is at once the danger and the value of Miss Stein's method. The value is that she does show us the identity of words, deprived of their old smothering associations. Of course, every accomplished writer does this to some degree. But Miss Stein goes further than most writers. At the same time, we see objects afresh.

The child and the great artist—these alone receive the sensation fresh as it was at the beginning of the world.

HAROLD ACTON

"I was born in the twentieth century, which is closer to the ninth than the nineteenth, and I belong to no special movement. It is undeniable, however, that I love beauty," Acton wrote, defending himself as a self-proclaimed aesthete. His appreciation of beauty began early, in the elegant Florentine villa where he grew up, a world that extended through the aristocratic mansion and into staid, manicured gardens where he and his older brother spent idyllic days. Only in summer did he leave the boundaries of this sumptuous environment, when he and his family sought to escape the heat of Italy by visiting his grandparents in Chicago and Lake Geneva, Wisconsin. Though he "felt just as American as . . . English," his strongest childhood memories stem from the glistening villa La Pietra.

Between childhood and Oxford, Acton was cloistered in a private school near Wokingham, Berkshire. "My spirit rebelled and remained perverse until Oxford set me free," he wrote, for he was never comfortable with his contemporaries and scorned their pranks and games.

At Oxford he felt more home, although his admiration for the Sitwells and T. S. Eliot set him apart from the more conventional scholars. "Experiments with words fascinated me," he admitted, and there were only two writers who earned his complete admiration—Joyce and Gertrude Stein.

When he learned from Edith Sitwell that Stein was to visit England, he invited her to address the "Ordinary," Oxford's literary society. There was so much curiosity about the writer that Acton opened the lecture to non-members; the audience filled a large room and listened, rapt, as Stein recited "Composition As Explanation," "casting a spell with her litany."

"The illusion that we were living in a continuous present was certainly there," Acton remarked. "When the reading came to an end life moved considerably faster." She was furiously assaulted with questions as soon as she finished speaking, but she remained undaunted, answering them "in reassuring motherly tones, patting and soothing the obstreperous with gusty sallies. . . ." She completely charmed the skeptical and hostile, dispelling the popular image of her as "a mermaid swathed in tinsel, smoking drugged cigarettes." To Acton, she seemed rather like an Aztec priestess.

He visited her several times in Paris, where, Acton recalled, they talked of his writing, or of Modernity (it was her "religion . . . and she harboured a notion that Great Britain suffered from hardening of the arteries"), or, more likely, of China—Acton's obsession.

He speculated that Hans Christian Andersen's story, "The Emperor's Nightingale," first awakened in him an interest in China. In any case, the interest developed into "an innate love of China beyond rational analysis. . . . Until I went to China my life would not be integrated and I knew it."

Finally, in 1932, he stood on Chinese soil for the first time. "An immense calm descended on me. . . . I felt strangely at home." He lived in China for the next seven years, traveling, lecturing in English at Peking National University, writing. It was not until 1939, when the war spurred him to England to join the RAF, that he could bring himself to leave. In the years that followed he devoted much time to translating the plays of the Peking theater.

Though his love of things Chinese earned him a dubious reputation among many of his countrymen, Stein understood his passions. "Acton is now a Chinaman," she declared, ". . . I imagine he really does now really look and feel like a Chinaman. . . ." But his wide travels never took him to China again; instead, he returned to the villa La Pietra, to its garden, and to the "vanished period" to which he belonged.

🌿 *Harold Acton / from* Memoirs of An Aesthete

Bruised by the cold, we adjourned for a hearty luncheon at a Catalan *bistro* nearby where the Master was treated with becoming reverence. Though he let others do the talking he radiated contentment in a detached way special to celebrities. Dora Maar was a soothing presence, Marie-Laure an eloquent Muse. The Master purred. Gertrude Stein's name cropped up during the meal. She and Alice Toklas had just returned from exile in a taxi bearing her most cherished possession, Picasso's portrait of her painted in 1906—together with her white poodle Basket and a large store of edible provisions.

"Let's all go and see her," said the Master. So there was a grand reunion with everyone talking at once in the Rue Christine. Picasso hugged Gertrude like a beloved bolster. *"Et mon portrait?"* he asked with a sudden note of anxiety, as if it were a lucky talisman. How often had he raised that question since it had been painted? It was there waiting for him and he examined it minutely. "Ah, it is finer than I had dreamt," he said, embracing her again.

If only as a publicity agent Gertrude had brought him luck. Her brother Leo, who was as repetitive as he was deaf—there was a strong family likeness—had often told me that when he had bought the early Picassos "she pretended to have discovered" Gertrude had been furious with him for buying such daubs. Be that as it may, she had revised her first impression. Her article on

Picasso in *Camera Work* (August 1912) begins: "One whom some were certainly following was one who was completely charming." After repeating this sentence with minor variations she proceeds: "Some were certainly following and were certain that the one they were then following was one bringing out of himself then something that was coming to be a heavy thing, a solid thing and a complete thing." The theme of "something had been coming out of him" alternates with "This one had always been working"—yet "He was not ever completely working." The longest sentence in the article attempts to summarize his achievement: "This one was always having something that was coming out of this one that was a solid thing, a charming thing, a lovely thing, a perplexing thing, a disconcerting thing, an interesting thing, a disturbing thing, a repellent thing, a very pretty thing." Later, in her best known and most lucid *Autobiography of Alice B. Toklas,* she paid him the supreme compliment of bracketing him with herself as a "first class genius."

It was amusing to watch the geniuses together. Both were rugged and squarely built; both had short hair and might have been taken for Aztec Mexicans; but whereas Picasso was muscularly mobile Gertrude was dumpily static. Though fifteen years had passed since I had seen her and Alice Toklas I could detect little change except that Gertrude had become more aggressively American in idiom and the use of slang, which seemed odd considering that she had been an expatriate most of her life. We had many friends in common and I saw her often. If one respected her colossal ego she could be warmly sympathetic. Her attempt to revitalize language was chiefly remarkable for its pertinacity, but only a fraction of her sense of fun percolates into her writings. Here and there a phrase arrests one's attention, such as "Civilization begins with a rose," but how many pages of stuttering repetition must be negotiated in order to find a gem of this quality!

In *Composition as Explanation* she wrote: "For a very long time everybody refuses and then almost without a pause almost everybody accepts." Almost everybody had accepted Picasso as a painter, but I fear that Gertrude Stein's "continuous present" is already a thing of the past. Her *Three Lives* had influenced writers of Hemingway's generation.

Having complete faith in herself, she had some to spare for others. Her memory was retentive and she praised my long-forgotten fantasy, *Cornelian*. I might still become a good writer, she observed: I had plenty to say and could say it well if I forgot all about English literature and remembered that I was half-American. "Your next book," she added, "must be a book of memoirs." Eventually I took her advice. While she discoursed with much humour and sense in a placid voice Alice attended to domestic details, acted as interpreter and tactful go-between. Hemingway has hinted that Alice had a vicious side, but I never saw her other than gentle and devoted to Gertrude, whom she cosseted with creamy cakes.

I invited them to lunch with me at the Chatham and the Officers Club and in each place they created a sensation. John Cullen, who was often in the company of a pretty French girl—"they are pretty like orchids, not like primroses," he remarked of the women of Paris—was shocked by the extreme dowdiness of this elderly couple. Gertrude's billowing skirt was not low enough to hide a pair of woolen gaiters which fell about her ankles, and Alice, tiny and hunched beside her with a hooked nose and light moustache, reminded John of the maiden ladies who fusted at Bath or Cheltenham. Gertrude insisted on bringing her poodle Basket, which made them even more conspicuous among women who resembled sleek mannequins. But Gertrude carried her-

self with the assurance of a Cleopatra. John was soon
won over by their conversation and remarked: "I can
see that I shall be calling Miss Stein *'chère maîtresse'*
next time I see her." When he mentioned that Hemingway was in Paris, Alice Toklas, speaking for both of
them as usual, said the only thing they liked about him
was his good looks when they first knew him at the age
of twenty-four. They thought he had become hopelessly
commercialized. "But the *career,"* he once said to them.
It was always "the career . . ."

My American colleagues at the Chatham were thrilled
to meet her and in a very short time she was distributing
autographs in her sloping scrawl. This was my second
guest who was asked for an autograph in public. The
third was Norman Douglas in a Capri restaurant.
"Certainly not," he snapped. "Unless they're prepared
to pay me a fee. Never heard of such cheek. They'll be
forging my signature next. I've seen that happen before." Had he been asked personally he might have
obliged them, but they had sent the request by a waiter
he disliked. For Gertrude the request was an outward
and visible sign of her celebrity. Considering that she
seldom went out except to take Basket for a walk, her
intimate knowledge of other people's lives was astonish-
ing: she excelled in the analysis of human relationships,
yet her pen-portraits of Cocteau, Edith Sitwell and other
friends contain no trace of her psychological insight.
The repetition of "Needs be needs be needs be near"
conveys little of Cocteau whereas in conversation there
was some truth in her remark that he prided himself on
being eternally thirty.

An assiduous crony of hers was Thomas Whittemore,
the Bostonian professor so comically sketched by Evelyn
Waugh in *Remote People.* Although Berenson and
many scholars deemed him a pious fraud, he had been
responsible for the restoration of the Byzantine mosaics
at Hagia Sophia and other mosques in Istanbul and had

founded a Byzantine Institute in Paris which he had come to reopen. Under the Occupation it had become a shambles, he said, and he complained that the Ritz Hotel, where he was staying, was positively Siberian, and he kept running into that awful cad Hemingway (a fellow Ritzonian but not a Bostonian) who gave him the cold shivers. Recollecting the dire discomfort of his trip to the Abyssinian monastery of Debra Lebanos with Evelyn Waugh, I had to smile.

The professor was almost as enthusiastic about Gertrude as about Byzantium and his flattery warmed the cockles of her heart. His articulation was painfully deliberate, but there was an ironical gleam in his eye which belied his solemnity. He told me that he had started cleaning the mosaics of Hagia Sophia with very fine dental instruments: "I scraped them like ivory teeth with marvellous results." Whatever his shortcomings, he deserved credit for this achievement. He gave me to understand that it had largely been due to his friendship with Mustafa Kemal, whom he had been able to influence in many constructive ways.

I doubt if the G.I.s who flocked to visit Gertrude had perused her writings. For them she was one of the living monuments of Paris, and they were attracted to this elderly frump as if she were a glamorous film-star. She must have felt like one when she posed for their cameras in front of the Stars and Stripes. She also felt fiercely democratic. This intellectual *vivandière,* as Natalie Barney called her, showed them her pictures, watched their reactions, encouraged any signs of independence, and scolded those who were fixed in their ideas. They sat on the floor and looked up to her with ravenous reverence while she spoke on a wide variety of subjects in a vigorous monotone, reducing them to speechlessness. I often wondered if and how she would influence their lives when they returned to the United States. Once I heard her explain to them that in her opinion all modern painting was based on what Cézanne had failed to do, instead of on what he had nearly succeeded in doing. To show what he could not achieve had become Cézanne's obsession and that of his followers, who had originated a system of camouflage which had developed into an art in peace and in war. Her argument was ingenious, but somewhat abstruse for the ingenuous, who listened open-mouthed, an occasional tongue displacing a gob of chewing gum.

When they were not calling on Gertrude and Picasso they were lining up for Chanel 5, the only scent in constant demand for transatlantic sweethearts.

VIRGIL THOMSON

Virgil Thomson came to Paris on tour with the Harvard Glee Club and stayed to study music on a traveling fellowship. He became instantly Parisian. Paris, he decided, reminded him of Kansas City, containing "all possible elements" of life. He was enthusiastic about the abundance of talent and charm he found everywhere; about the restaurants and hotels decorated with "huge flattened flowers and jumpy stripes" as in the paintings of Henri Matisse; and about Gertrude Stein.

He was taken to her salon by the composer George Antheil, and although Alice Toklas' first impression of him was cool, he and Gertrude "got on like Harvard men." Later he admitted being "struck by the intensity with which Miss Stein and I took each other up. From the fall of 1926, in fact, till her death in July of 1946, we were forever loving being together, whether talking and walking, writing to each other, or at work."

The work revolved around the setting to music of *Four Saints In Three Acts* and, later, *The Mother of Us All*. The theme for *Four Saints* was mutually conceived. After the libretto was complete, Thomson created a score that gave "musical reinforcement" to Stein's words—to the writing which was "closer to musical timings than to speech timings," according to Thomson. He also composed music for "Susie Asado,"

"Preciosilla," "Portrait of F. B." and "Capital Capitals."

Four Saints was originally produced in Hartford, Connecticut, in 1933 and traveled to New York and then to Chicago, where Miss Stein attended a performance during her American lecture tour. There was some dispute about the splitting of profits: she wanted a fifty-fifty division; he felt he deserved two-thirds but eventually gave in. "For Gertrude, about money, did not joke," he came to realize.

Gertrude Stein's influence did not end with her collaboration on the operettas. Thomson, a pioneer in his own medium, took her methods of portraiture and applied it to music. His portraits were "an exercise not only in objectivity but also in avoiding the premeditated." His subjects were as diverse as Picasso, Aaron Copland and Fiorello La Guardia.

Some years after they worked together on *Four Saints,* Stein presented the composer with *The Mother of Us All,* her opera based on the life of Susan B. Anthony. It opened, after Miss Stein's death, at Columbia University in 1947.

"In setting the Stein texts to music," Thomson wrote, "I had in mind the acoustical support of a trajectory, of a verbal volubility that would brook no braking." In realizing his goal, he added a new dimension to the work of Gertrude Stein.

❧ *Virgil Thomson / from* Virgil Thomson

Gertrude Stein in her younger days had liked to write all night and sleep all day. She also, it seems, ate copiously, drank wine, and smoked cigars. By the time I knew her, at fifty-two, she ate abstemiously; she neither drank nor smoked; and she was likely to wake, as people do in middle life, by nine. Her volume had been diminished too. Her appearance, nevertheless, on account of low stature (five feet, two), remained monumental, like that of some saint or sibyl sculpted three-fourths life size. Her working powers also were intact, remained so, indeed, until her death at seventy-two.

Actually a whole domestic routine had been worked out for encouraging those powers to function daily. In the morning she would read, write letters, play with the dog, eventually bathe, dress, and have her lunch. In the afternoon she drove in the car, walked, window-shopped, spent a litle money. She did nothing by arrangement till after four. At some point in her day she always wrote; and since she waited always for the moment when she would be full of readiness to write, what she wrote came out of fullness as an overflowing.

Year round, these routines varied little, except that in the country, if there were house guests, excursions by car might be a little longer, tea or lunch taken out instead of at home. When alone and not at work, Gertrude would walk, read, or meditate. She loved to walk; and she consumed books by the dozen, sent to her when away from home by the American Library in Paris. She read English and American history, memoirs, minor

123

literature from the nineteenth century, crime fiction, rarely modern art-writing, and never the commercial magazines. When people were around she would talk and listen, ask questions. She talked with anybody and everybody. When exchanging news and views with neighbors, concierges, policemen, shop people, garage men, hotel servants, she was thoroughly interested in them all. Gertrude not only liked people, she needed them. They were grist for her poetry, a relief from the solitudes of a mind essentially introspective.

Alice Toklas neither took life easy nor fraternized casually. She got up at six and cleaned the drawing room herself, because she did not wish things broken. (Porcelain and other fragile objects were her delight, just as pictures were Gertrude's; and she could imagine using violence toward a servant who might break one.) She liked being occupied, anyway, and did not need repose, ever content to serve Gertrude or be near her. She ran the house, ordered the meals, cooked on occasion, and typed out everything that got written into the blue copybooks that Gertrude had adopted from French school children. From 1927 or '28 she also worked petit point, matching in silk the colors and shades of designs made especially for her by Picasso. These tapestries were eventually applied to a pair of Louis XV small armchairs (*chauffeuses*) that Gertrude had bought for her. She was likely, any night, to go to bed by eleven, while Miss Stein would sit up late if there were someone to talk with.

Way back before World War I, in 1910 or so, in Granada, Gertrude had experienced the delights of writing directly in the landscape. This does not mean just working out of doors; it means being surrounded by the thing one is writing about at the time one is writing about it. Later, in 1924, staying at Saint-Rémy in Provence, and sitting in fields beside the irrigation ditches, she found the same sound of running water as in Granada to soothe her while she wrote or while she simply sat, imbuing herself with the landscape's sight and sound. In the country around Belley, where she began to summer only a few years later, she wrote *Lucy Church Amiably* wholly to the sound of streams and waterfalls.

Bravig Imbs, an American poet and novelist who knew her in the late twenties, once came upon her doing this. The scene took place in a field, its enactors being Gertrude, Alice, and a cow. Alice, by means of a stick, would drive the cow around the field. Then, at a sign from Gertrude, the cow would be stopped; and Gertrude would write in her copybook. After a bit, she would pick up her folding stool and progress to another spot, whereupon Alice would again start the cow moving around the field till Gertrude signaled she was ready to write again. Though Alice now says that Gertrude drove the cow, she waiting in the car, the incident, whatever its choreography, reveals not only Gertrude's working intimacy with landscape but also the concentration of two friends on an act of composition by one of them that typifies and reveals their daily life for forty years. Alice had decided long before that "Gertrude was always right," that she was to have whatever she wanted when she wanted it, and that the way to keep herself always wanted was to keep Gertrude's writing always and forever unhindered, unopposed.

Gertrude's preoccupation with painting and painters was not shared by Alice except in so far as certain of Gertrude's painter friends touched her heart, and Picasso was almost the only one of these. Juan Gris was another, and Christian Bérard a very little bit. But Matisse I know she had not cared for, nor Braque. If it had not been for Gertrude, I doubt that Alice would ever have had much to do with the world of painting. She loved objects and furniture, practiced cooking and gardening, understood music. Of music, indeed, she had a long experience, having once, as a young girl, played a piano concerto in public. But painting was less absorbing to her than to Gertrude.

Gertrude's life with pictures seems to have begun as a preoccupation shared with her brothers, Michael and Leo. The sculptor Jacques Lipchitz once remarked to me the miraculous gift of perception by which these young Californians, in Paris of the 1900s, had gone straight to the cardinal values. Virtually without technical experience (since only Leo, among them, had painted at all) and without advice (for there were no modern-art scholars then), they bought Cézanne, Matisse, and Picasso. In quantity and, of course, for almost nothing. But also, according to Lipchitz, the Steins' taste was strongest when they bought together. Gertrude and Leo did this as long as they lived together, which was till about 1911. Michael, who had started quite early buying Matisses, kept that up till World War I. After Gertrude and Leo separated, she made fewer purchases and no major ones at all, save some Juan Gris canvases that represented a continuing commitment to Spanish cubism and to friendship. She could no longer buy Picasso or Cézanne after their prices got high, or after she owned a car. But throughout the twenties and thirties she was always looking for new painters, without being able to commit herself to any of them till she discovered about 1929 Sir Francis Rose. From him she quickly acquired nearly a hundred pictures, and she insisted till her death that he was a great painter. No other collector, no museum, no international dealer has yet gone so far.

Looking at painting had been for Gertrude Stein a nourishment throughout the late twenties and thirties of her own life. She never ceased to state her debt to Cézanne, for it was from constantly gazing on a portrait by him that she had found her way into and through the vast maze of motivations and proclivities that make up the patterns of people and types of people in *Three Lives* and in *The Making of Americans*. "The wonderful thing about Cézanne," she would say, "is that he was never tempted." Gertrude Stein's biographers have stated that Picasso also was a source for her and that in *Tender Buttons* she was endeavoring to reproduce with words the characteristic devices of cubist painting. There may even be in existence a quotation from Gertrude herself to this effect. But she certainly did not repeat it the way she loved to repeat her allegiance to Cézanne. I myself have long doubted the validity, or at any rate the depth, of such a statement. An influence of poetry on painting is quite usual, a literary theme being illustrated by images. But any mechanism by which this procedure might be reversed and painting come to influence literature (beyond serving as subject for a review) is so rare a concept that the mere statement of Gertrude Stein's intent to receive such an influence surely requires fuller explanation. Let us try.

First of all, *Tenders Buttons,* subtitled "Objects . . . Food . . . Rooms," is an essay in description, of which the subjects are those commonly employed by painters of still life. And cubist painting too was concerned with still life. Cubism's characteristic device in representing still life was to eliminate the spatially fixed viewpoint, to see around corners, so to speak, to reduce its subject to essentials of form and profile and then to reassemble these as a summary or digest of its model. Resemblance was not forbidden; on the contrary, clues were offered to help the viewer recognize the image; and cubist painters (from the beginning, according to Gertrude) had been disdainful of viewers who could not "read" their canvases. (Today's "abstract" painters, on the other hand, maintain that in their work resemblances are purely accidental.)

According to Alice Toklas, the author's aim in *Tender Buttons* was "to describe something without mentioning

127

it." Sometimes the name of the object is given in a title, sometimes not; but each description is full of clues, some of them easy to follow up, others put there for throwing you off the scent. All are legitimately there, however, since in Blake's words, "everything possible to be believed is an image of truth," and since in Gertrude Stein's method anything that comes to one in a moment of concentrated working is properly a part of the poem. Nevertheless, unveiling the concealed image is somewhat more difficult to a reader of *Tender Buttons* than to the viewer of a cubist still life. For a still life is static; nothing moves in it; time is arrested. In literature, on the other hand, one word comes after another and the whole runs forward. To have produced static pictures in spite of a non-fixed eye-point was cubism's triumph, just as giving the illusion of movement within a framed picture was the excitement of vorticism, as in Marcel Duchamp's *Nude Descending a Staircase*. To have described objects, food, and rooms both statically and dynamically, with both a painter's eye and a poet's continuity, gives to *Tender Buttons* its particular brilliance, its way of both standing still and moving forward.

Now the carrier of that motion, make no mistake, is a rolling eloquence in no way connected with cubism. This eloquence, in fact, both carries forward the description and defeats it, just as in cubist painting description was eventually defeated by the freedom of the painter (with perspective making no demands) merely to create a composition. Cubism was always, therefore, in danger of going decorative (hence flat); and the kind of writing I describe here could just as easily turn into mere wit and oratory. That cubism was something of an impasse its short life, from 1909 to 1915, would seem to indicate; and there were never more than two possible exits from it. One was complete concealment of the image, hence in effect its elimination; the other was retreat into naturalism. Both paths have been followed in our time, though not by Picasso, who has avoided abstraction as just another trap leading to the decorative, and who could never bring himself, for mere depiction, to renounce the ironic attitudes involved in voluntary stylization.

Gertrude, faced with two similar paths, chose both. During the years between 1927 and '31, she entered into an involvement with naturalism that produced at the end of her life *Yes Is for a Very Young Man, Brewsie and Willie,* and *The Mother of Us All,* each completely clear and in no way mannered. She was also during those same years pushing abstraction farther than it had ever gone before, not only in certain short pieces still completely hermetic (even to Alice Toklas), but in extended studies of both writing and feeling in which virtually everything remains obscure but the mood, works such as "As a Wife Has a Cow, a Love Story"; "Patriarchal Poetry"; and "Stanzas in Meditation."

Her last operas and plays are in the humane tradition of letters, while her monumental abstractions of the late 1920s and early 1930s are so intensely aware of both structure and emotion that they may well be the origin of a kind of painting that came later to be known as "abstract expressionism." If this be true, then Gertrude Stein, after borrowing from cubism a painting premise, that of the non-fixed viewpoint, returned that premise to its origins, transformed. Whether the transformation could have been operated within painting itself, without the help of a literary example, we shall never know, because the literary example was there. We do know, however, that no single painter either led that transformation or followed it through as a completed progress in his own work.

Gertrude had been worried about painting ever since cubism had ceased to evolve. She did not trust abstraction in art, which she found constricted between flat color schemes and pornography. Surrealism, for her taste, was too arbitrary as to theme and too poor as painting. And she could not give her faith to the neo-Romantics either, though she found Bérard "alive" and "the best" of them. She actually decided in 1928 that "painting [had] become a minor art again," meaning without nourishment for her. Then within the year, she had found Francis Rose. What nourishment she got from him I cannot dream, nor did she ever speak of him save as a gifted one destined to lead his art—an English leader this time, instead of Spanish.

In her own work, during these late twenties, while still developing ideas received from Picasso, she was also moving into new fields opened by her friendship with me. I do not wish to pretend that her ventures into romantic feeling, into naturalism, autobiography, and the opera came wholly through me, though her discovery of the opera as a poetic form certainly did. Georges Hugnet, whom I had brought to her, was at least equally a stimulation, as proved by her "translation" of one of his extended works. She had not previously accepted, since youth, the influence of any professional writer. Her early admiration for Henry James and Mark Twain had long since become a reflex. She still remembered Shakespeare of the sonnets, as "Stanzas in Meditation" will show; and she considered Richardson's *Clarissa Harlowe* (along with *The Making of Americans*) to be "the other great novel in English." But for "movements" and their organizers in contemporary poetry she had the greatest disdain—for Pound, Eliot, Yeats, and their volunteer militiamen. She admitted Joyce to be "a good writer," disclaimed any influence on her from his work, and believed, with some evidence, that she had influenced him.

She knew that in the cases of Sherwood Anderson and Ernest Hemingway her influence had gone to them, not theirs to her. I do not know the real cause of her break with Hemingway, only that after a friendship of several years she did not see him any more and declared forever after that he was "yellow." Anderson remained a friend always, though I do not think she ever took him seriously as a writer. The poet Hart Crane she did take seriously. And there were French young men, René Crevel, for one, whom she felt tender about and whom Alice adored. Cocteau amused her as a wit and as a dandy, less so as an organizer of epochs, a role she had come to hold in little respect from having known in prewar times Guillaume Apollinaire, whom she esteemed low as a poet, even lower as a profiteer of cubism. Pierre de Massot she respected as a prose master; but he was too French, too violent, to touch her deeply. Gide and Jouhandeau, making fiction out of sex, she found as banal as any titillater of chambermaids. Max Jacob she had disliked personally from the time of his early friendship with Picasso. I never heard her express any opinion of him as a writer, though Alice says now that she admired him.

In middle life she had come at last to feel about her own work that it "could be compared to the great poetry of the past." And if she was nearly alone during her lifetime in holding this view (along with Alice Toklas, myself, and perhaps a very few more), she was equally alone in having almost no visible poetic parents or progeny. Her writing seemed to come from nowhere and to influence, at that time, none but reporters and novelists. She herself, considering the painter Cézanne her chief master, believed that under his silent tutelage a major message had jumped like an electric arc from painting to poetry. And she also suspected that its high tension was in process of short-circuiting again, from her through me, this time to music. I do not offer this theory as my own, merely as a thought thrown out by Gertrude Stein to justify, perhaps, by one more case the passing of an artistic truth or method which she felt strongly to have occurred for her, across one of those distances that lie between sight, sound, and words.

There was nevertheless, in Alice Toklas, literary influence from a nonprofessional source. As early as 1910, in a narrative called "Ada," later published in *Geography and Plays,* a piece which recounts Miss Toklas's early life, Gertrude imitated Alice's way of telling a story. This sentence is typical: "He had a pleasant life while he was living and after he was dead his wife and children remembered him." Condensation in this degree was not Gertrude's way; expansion through repetition (what she called her "garrulity") was more natural to her. But she could always work from an auditory model, later in *Brewsie and Willie* transcribing almost literally the usage and syntax of World War II American soldiers. And having mastered a new manner by imitating Alice Toklas in "Ada," she next mixed it with her repetitive manner in a story called "Miss Furr and Miss Skeen." Then she set aside the new narrative style for nearly thirty years.

In 1933 she took it up again for writing *The Autobiography of Alice B. Toklas,* which is the story of her own life told in Miss Toklas's words. This book is in every way except actual authorship Alice Toklas's book; it reflects her mind, her language, her private view of Gertrude, also her unique narrative powers. Every story in it is told as Alice herself had always told it. And when in 1961 Miss Toklas herself wrote *What Is Remembered,* she told her stories with an even greater brevity. There is nothing comparable to this compactness elsewhere in English, nor to my knowledge in any other literature, save possibly in Julius Caesar's *De bello Gallico.* Gertrude imitated it three times with striking success. She could not use it often, because its way was not hers.

Her own way with narrative was ever elliptical, going into slow orbit around her theme. Alice's memory and interests were visual; she could recall forever the exact costumes people had worn, where they had stood or sat, the décor of a room, the choreography of an occasion. Gertrude's memory was more for the sound of a voice, for accent, grammar, and vocabulary. And even these tended to grow vague in one day, because her sustained curiosity about what had happened lay largely in the possibilities of any incident for revealing character.

How often have I heard her begin some tale, a recent one or a far-away one, and then as she went on with it get first repetitive and then uncertain till Alice would look up over the tapestry frame and say, "I'm sorry, Lovey; it wasn't like that at all." "All right, Pussy," Gertrude would say. "You tell it." Every story that ever came into the house eventually got told in Alice's way, and this was its definitive version. The accounts of life in the country between 1942 and 1945 that make up *Wars I Have Seen* seem to me, on the other hand, Gertrude's own; I find little of Alice in them. Then how are they so vivid? Simply from the fact, or at least so I imagine, that she would write in the evening about what she had seen that day, describe events while their memory was still fresh.

Gertrude's artistic output has the quality, rare in our century, of continuous growth. Picasso had evolved rapidly through one discovery after another until the cubist time was over. At that point, in 1915, he was only thirty-three and with a long life to be got through. He has got through it on sheer professionalism—by inventing tricks and using them up (tricks mostly recalling the history of art or evoking historic Spanish art), by watching the market very carefully (collecting his own pictures), and by keeping himself advised about trends in literary content and current-events content. But his major painting was all done early. Igor Stravinsky followed a similar pattern. After giving to the world between 1909 and 1913 three proofs of colossally expanding power—*The Firebird, Petrouchka,* and *The Rite of Spring*—he found himself at thirty-one unable to expand farther. And since, like Picasso, he was still to go on living, and since he could not imagine living without making music, he too was faced with an unhappy choice. He would either make music out of his own past (which he disdained to do) or out of music's past (which he is still doing). For both men, when expansion ceased, working methods became their subject.

One could follow this design through many careers in music, painting, and poetry. Pound, I think, continued to develop; Eliot, I should say, did not. Arnold Schoenberg was in constant evolution; his chief pupils, Alban Berg and Anton Webern, were more static. The last two were saved by early death from possible decline of inspiration, just as James Joyce's approaching blindness concentrated and extended his high period for twenty years, till he had finished two major works, *Ulysses* and *Finnegans Wake.* He died fulfilled, exhausted, but lucky in the sense that constant growth had not been expected of him. Indeed, for all that the second of these two works is more complex than the first, both in concept and in language, it does not represent a growth in anything but mastery. Joyce was a virtuoso type, like Picasso, of whom Max Jacob, Picasso's friend from earliest youth, had said, "Always he escapes by acrobatics." And virtuosos do not grow; they merely become more skillful. At least they do not grow like vital organisms, but rather, like crystals, reproduce their characteristic forms.

Gertrude Stein's maturation was more like that of Arnold Schoenberg. She ripened steadily, advanced slowly from each stage to the next. She had started late, after college and medical school. From *Three Lives,* begun in 1904 at thirty, through *The Making of Americans,* finished in 1911, her preoccupation is character analysis. From *Tender Buttons* (1912) to "Patriarchal

Poetry" (1927) a quite different kind of writing is presented (not, of course, without having been prefigured). This is hermetic to the last degree, progressing within its fifteen-year duration from picture-words and rolling rhetoric to syntactical complexity and neutral words. From 1927 to 1934 two things go on at once. There are long hermetic works (*Four Saints, Lucy Church Amiably,* and "Stanzas in Meditation") but also straightforward ones like *The Autobiography of Alice B. Toklas* and the lectures on writing. After her return in 1935 from the American lecture tour, hermetic writing gradually withers and the sound of spoken English becomes her theme, giving in *Yes Is for a Very Young Man,* in *The Mother of Us All,* and in *Brewsie and Willie* vernacular portraits of remarkable veracity.

Her development had not been aided or arrested by public success, of which there had in fact been very little. The publication of *Three Lives* in 1909 she had subsidized herself, as she did in 1922 that of the miscellany *Geography and Plays. The Making of Americans,* published by McAlmon's Contact Editions in 1925, was her first book-size book to be issued without her paying for it; and she was over fifty. She had her first bookstore success at fifty-nine with the *Autobiography.* When she died in 1946, at seventy-two, she had been working till only a few months before without any diminution of power. Her study of technical problems never ceased; never had she felt obliged to fabricate an inspiration; and she never lost her ability to speak from the heart.

Gertrude lived by the heart, indeed; and domesticity was her theme. Not for her the matings and rematings that went on among the amazons. An early story from 1903, published after her death, *Things as They Are,* told of one such intrigue in post-Radcliffe days. But after 1907 her love life was serene, and it was Alice Toklas who made it so. Indeed, it was this tranquil life

that offered to Gertrude a fertile soil of sentiment-
security in which other friendships great and small
could come to flower, wither away, be watered, cut off,
or preserved in a book. Her life was like that of a child,
to whom danger can come only from the outside, never
from home, and whose sole urgency is growth. It was
also that of an adult who demanded all the rights of a
man along with the privileges of a woman.

Just as Gertrude kept up friendships among the
amazons, though she did not share their lives, she held
certain Jews in attachment for their family-like warmth,
though she felt no solidarity with Jewry. Tristan Tzara
—French-language poet from Romania, Dada pioneer,
early surrealist, and battler for the Communist party—
she said was "like a cousin." Miss Etta and Dr. Claribel
Cone, picture buyers and friends from Baltimore days,
she handled almost as if they were her sisters. The
sculptors Jo Davidson and Jacques Lipchitz, the painter
Man Ray she accepted as though they had a second
cousin's right to be part of her life. About men or
goyim, even about her oldest man friend, Picasso, she
could feel unsure; but a woman or a Jew she could size
up quickly. She accepted without cavil, indeed, all the
conditionings of her Jewish background. And if, as she
would boast, she was "a bad Jew," she at least did not
think of herself as Christian. Of heaven and salvation
and all that she would say, "When a Jew dies he's
dead." We used to talk a great deal, in fact, about our
very different religious conditionings, the subject having
come up through my remarking the frequency with
which my Jewish friends would break with certain of
theirs and never make up. Gertrude's life had contained
many people that she still spoke of (Mabel Dodge, for
instance) but from whom she refused all communication. The Stettheimers' conversation was also full of
references to people they had known well but did not
wish to know any more. And I began to imagine this

definitiveness about separations as possibly a Jewish trait. I was especially struck by Gertrude's rupture with her brother Leo, with whom she had lived for many years in intellectual and no doubt affectionate communion, but to whom she never spoke again after they had divided their pictures and furniture, taken up separate domiciles.

The explanation I offered for such independent behavior was that the Jewish religion, though it sets aside a day for private Atonement, offers no mechanics for forgiveness save for offenses against one's own patriarch, and even he is not obliged to pardon. When a Christian, on the other hand, knows he has done wrong to anyone, he is obliged in all honesty to attempt restitution; and the person he has wronged must thereupon forgive. So that if Jews seem readier to quarrel than to make up, that fact seems possibly to be the result of their having no confession-and-forgiveness formula, whereas Christians, who experience none of the embarrassment that Jews find in admitting misdeeds, arrange their lives, in consequence, with greater flexibility, though possibly, to a non-Christian view, with less dignity.

Gertrude liked this explanation, and for nearly twenty years it remained our convention. It was not till after her death that Alice said one day,

You and Gertrude had it settled between you as to why Jews don't make up their quarrels, and I went along with you. But now I've found a better reason for it. Gertrude was right, of course, to believe that "when a Jew dies he's dead." And that's exactly why Jews don't need to make up. When we've had enough of someone we can get rid of him. You Christians can't, because you've got to spend eternity together.

FRANCIS ROSE

The thunderstorm that raged during Francis Rose's birth on September 18, 1909, was characteristic of his tumultuous youth. Life in his aristocratic English family was marked by his mother's eccentricities, which became full-blown after his father's death. She became obsessed with spiritualism, often falling into trances, rushing to her son's bedside and giving him messages in his father's voice. His grandmother was his close companion, intermittently acting as tutor between the comings and goings of various French governesses, and he accompanied her on many trips abroad. Soon Paris was as familiar to him as his native London.

He began painting as a young child, knowing at once that it was all he ever wanted to do. "All my childhood memories," he later wrote, "were of seeing things, some ugly, some beautiful, some immeasurably gay, and some so very, very sad. I saw colour and, most of all, shapes and flat and combined surfaces." As a boy, the art world he knew was presided over by Aubrey Beardsley, Oscar Wilde, Huysmans—artists very different from those he would meet later in Paris.

A willful child, indulged by his family, Francis Rose frequently ran away from home, feeling even as a youth that "life must be lived till its seams were bursting." He marked the beginning of his real life—a full adult life—as 1925, when he visited his mother's villa in Villefranche and met Jean Cocteau and Christian Bérard. He was quickly taken into the avant-garde circle that clustered around Cocteau, discovering there the benefits of opium and the torments of being an artist.

Predictably, he went on to Paris and took up residence in Montmartre, where he covered the walls of one room with tarred black paper and the windows with black oilcloth curtains. The smell of tar, he maintained, excited his imagination. There he tried to achieve his artistic goal of producing "the simplest truths . . . those which are the least obvious to the eyes and the most important to the inside of the picture."

He came to know Francis Picabia, "a better teacher than an artist," he thought; through Picabia he eventually met Gertrude Stein.

Miss Stein had already purchased several of Rose's paintings at a Paris gallery and, although she had not been overenthusiastic about meeting a new artist, found Francis Rose "elegant, unbalanced and intelligent. . . ." For a long while she maintained that he was "the only interesting one among the young men painting."

During his visits to Gertrude Stein's residences in Paris and Bilignin, he won not only her esteem but her affection. He was, she said, like all the Francises she knew, "very beautiful to hear, to see and to do." And for him she was "a great mind who helped to build the twentieth century . . . writer and inventor of the new American language. . . ."

🌿 *Francis Rose / from* Saying Life

After Mother had died I tried to escape from the tragic cycle that had already started to surround me, and went to Paris again. This time it was autumn. Méraud and Chili Guevara had arrived a few days before me and were living in a round ivy-covered house near the Boulevard Montparnasse. It was a Victorian faked mediaeval tower, and it was here that I was to meet Gertrude Stein and Alice B. Toklas for the first time.

It was late afternoon; it was tea-time. A noise as of wild caged animals greeted me in the hall as the door was opened. Soon the source of the noise became apparent for Chili pushed me into the drawing-room. A big black and white spotted dog was chasing a little dog, and a very big white poodle chased the spotted dog, and another dog chased the poodle, and round and round the room they went, and Méraud was shouting and people were struggling as people will struggle when dogs are fighting and everybody was being aimlessly agitated and perturbed: that is, everyone who was on his feet, for one woman sat at the table in the middle of the room quietly eating a cake. She had her back to me, and her hair which was turning grey was cut very short.

As Chili was a little perturbed at having to receive a new guest and attend to a dog fight at the same moment, he took the easy course and pushed me into a seat next to the woman with the cake, mumbling something quite incomprehensible. The cake slowly disappeared, the dog fight was over, and the woman turned to me and said,

"You are Francis Rose?" I said "Yes." "Do you want to see your pictures?" I felt very surprised and said yes. "Well, later," she replied. These were the first words I exchanged with Gertrude Stein, before I knew who she was. Then Méraud told me, and I met Alice too, Since then I have loved them. I met Basket also—the first Basket—and Basket was the first poodle, the champion of the noise. It was Basket who had brought about Gertrude Stein's purchase of her first painting by me. She had visited Jean Bonjean's gallery near the vet who was bathing and clipping Basket from the French style of dressing a poodle. All summer he had been allowed to go wild in the fields around Bilignin: a small gentleman's residence of the early eighteenth century near Belley in the Department of Ain.

Until that tea party I did not know that Gertrude had bought pictures of mine, so it was on this memorable day that my work and life became first connected with her. She did not talk much then but other people did . . and when the talking was over we walked across the Boulevard Raspail to the rue de Fleurus.

I was ignorant then about the rue de Fleurus. I did not know of the great glamour that it held for artists, for the great and famous, for, above all, the inquisitive young, the wild, the violent, and the creative who had crossed its threshold, drunk Alice's wonderful tea, and eaten her exotic petit-fours. I came to it as to just a new house; the street was just a most ordinary Paris street, not one of the beautiful ones of the Rive Gauche. We went through a *porte-cochère* with a shabby concierge's lodge in which sat an old concierge wearing a postman's cap and blue workman's trousers; the small flagged courtyard we crossed was shabbier still, and facing us was a large lock-up studio which might have been a garage or workshop with a small residence attached.

The studio was higher than it was wide; the furniture was heavy and Renaissance; a great sofa and armchairs

stuffed with horse-hair filled the middle; two tiny
Louis XV chairs stood nearby; they were covered with
jewel-like petit-point tapestry, one in bright yellow,
black, and red, the other in green and white. These were
the work of Alice Toklas from the designs Picasso had
painted on the canvas. The atmosphere was like that of
a cultured Spanish house—but the walls! The walls
were covered tier over tier with paintings, one over the
other until one could hardly see them near the ceiling.
Paintings of the kind that only people who love paint
will have. I do not mean pictures. I think that when
Gertrude Stein wrote her essay on painting she expressed this when she said she loved painting, all painting on flat surfaces and in oil paint. Indeed, oil paint,
and particularly white oil paint, delighted her, most of
all that used by Spanish painters. Another thing she
liked was *trompe-l'oeil*. She had discovered in Italy that
if she were especially pleased with the marble in some
church, it always turned out to be real marble mixed
up with a painted imitation. And a curtain or shutters
depicted on a wall gave her more pleasure than the
real thing, although she never discovered why.

At this period I felt that abstract painting was really
the most photographic form of art, as had been proved
by Picasso's discovery of cubism in the construction
and composition of Spanish landscapes and which
Braque had sung about in paint; as a kind of com-
mentary of French thought on this subject, cubism had
always existed, but only Paolo Uccello and Picasso
really knew how to use it. The phrase "revolution in
art" is only relative, as it means catholic or universal
rather than orthodox, and I was looking for something
nearer the real, the non-figurative, and the Chinese eye
for painting. I was feeling my ground carefully, therefore surrealism could not be a real revolution to me. The
real revolution has always been hidden in the marvellous and in the undefinable in painting: a dimension

seen by Leonardo da Vinci, a truth expressed by Piero
della Francesca, a piece of magic in oil paint by Rem-
brandt, the hideousness of an imaginary world by
Bosch, the jewelry which Holbein used to lead up to
the face in his English portraits, the purity of bad taste
in Ingres, and many other miracles in the art of making
pictures. Literature does not count in painting as literary
ideas destroy painting. I love paint, and all forms of
making paint live, as much by its medium as by any
idea expressed in a picture. I have painted either with
violence or with softness, and generally there are no
tricks in my work for critics to hook their intelligence
onto. It was Miró and Paul Klee who interested me
most.

I had forgotten the pictures I had left with Bonjean
because I desired to forget Brittany. The model who
had posed for the big man on a blue ground which
Gertrude Stein had bought had died of yellow fever in
the Belgian Congo. It was the largest portrait I had so
far painted, and it still hangs in Gertrude Stein's dining-
room in the rue Christine in Paris. Kit Wood, too, had
killed himself, and Diaghilev had died.

On my first visit to the famous studio in the rue de
Fleurus, the *Femme au chapeau* of Matisse had gone
with the Renoirs in the division of the collection when
Gertrude Stein's brother, Leo, had left her, and she
and Alice Toklas had made up their minds which
pictures they would keep. I am often sad that the *Femme au chapeau* went to Leo as it looked like Alice
Toklas and the great painted hat must have been almost
symbolic of Alice, who loved hats, when Gertrude had
bought it in the *Salon d'Automne*.

It is rare in a human life when one can see the
greatest paintings of the period hanging in one room,
with a great personality standing next to one—a personality who had bought them as unknown works by
artists considered doubtful painters by the critics. For

143

the love of pictures, Gertrude had bought the paintings
which she loved. It was like being next to the Count
Duke de Olivares when the recently finished works of
Velázquez hung on his austere whitewashed walls and
his quill was still in his hand after writing the final
synopsis of his views in Torre.

On entering the studio for the first time, I immediately noticed an ostrich egg made into a lamp with the
shade of Negro raffia-work, and, next to it, an egg-cup
and spoon cast in lead, painted with dots. It was the
first sculpture *collage,* made by Picasso. Then my eye
was caught by the painting, and the first one to strike
me was not my own, although I saw them somewhere
in the background of my visual sensibility, but Picasso's
Femme au pannier of the blue period. It was a frail
girl with black hair and a basket of red flowers and it
was like a real little girl. Next I noticed a stronger nude
in pinks where Picasso had said so much and so little
and was thinking of Negro sculpture. Above this painting hung a picture of prostitutes at a bar, a weaker
but magnificent effort to break away from the atmosphere of Toulouse-Lautrec's Paris and bring it to
Barcelona. This now belongs to Chester Dale. The
paintings I noticed with most intensity were a realistic
colour study of an apple by Picasso which exceeded
Cézanne's best paintings of the same subject; his
studies in lines and strokes of colour for *Les demoiselles
d'Avignon,* a Negro head and *L'étudiant.* The portrait
by Picasso meant less to me, as it was brown in colour
and seemed to be a pair with Cézanne's portrait of
his wife. *L'étudiant, My Julie,* and *L'Harlequin* by
Picasso struck me as great paintings. In tearing a piece
of brown packing paper, Picasso had created a cap
for his student which had the importance that only
Cranach could give to a hat relative to a face or a nude.
The little *Baigneurs* by Cézanne glittered like a jewel,
and Juan Gris' roses in *collage* and *nature morte* had

the clearness of a section of living vision cut out with sharp scissors. These great paintings of Gris were so clean and yet so undecorative that I felt I was in Sierra Madre, Elche, and the cord-maker's caves at Crevillente at the same time.

Next to these pictures hung three rows of my paintings which made me feel bewildered and alone; I had forgotten painting most of these pictures, and nothing is more tiresome for an artist than seeing his finished works. The shepherd sleeping in the ruins painted in 1928 on absorbent board, the little chair painted in 1929, Byron meditating, the big blue man, *L'Italienne,* a fog at sea, and a river in Spain (which was painted in Brittany)—in fact I cannot remember all my pictures that were there.

Gertrude Stein told me that I had been described to her by Virgil Thomson, but like all musicians' descriptions his was wrong. She did not want to meet a new painter, but now that it had happened we had to meet again. People's private lives were beginning to bore her and she called for Alice for consultation.."Yes," Alice agreed, "Francis Rose must come again." Miss Stein talked to me about my work and gave me the following advice: I must work more and even more, I must have an exhibition, and I must consider my work to be very serious. I must realize that my painting must come first and that I could not afford to be silly in my life. All this did me good, although I could not help feeling afraid of meeting Gertrude again. I felt that I should not have met her and that she should only have known of my work. How could I ever get to know this woman? She seemed so strong, so detached, and so direct; but I was wrong, yes, really wrong, for from the day we met, notwithstanding one quarrel, Gertrude Stein was to remain my most loyal friend. As a person she took the place of my mother, and as an unwavering supporter of my painting I think that she was the only person who ever really understood my own revolution.

When I told my friends that I had met Gertrude, they laughed and said, "Well, that will be the end of you, at twenty-seven rue de Fleurus! The same thing will happen to you as happened to Pavel Tchelitchew, Christian Tony, the Berman brothers, Christian Bérard, and many others." Pavel Tchelitchew had been thrown out of the house by Alice Toklas because he had painted a picture—I believe it was a portrait of Edith Sitwell—which Gertrude did not like, and he had made a scene when she had refused to admire it. Tony and the Bermans had been discarded for some reason which I have forgotten. Bébé Bérard Gertrude had found too clever, altogether too mundane and delightful. She had said to him, "I like you, Bébé, but you are not *sérieux* about your painting. It is all too facile—and so good-bye." Even her great friend Virgil Thomson, after boring her with a love story, had received a Christmas card wishing him all happiness and love, but requesting him not to call any more at 27 rue Fleurus—fortunately this rupture was short-lived. All this frightened me, I was well-acquainted with the sharp tongues of the little band which surrounded Jean Cocteau, but on account of my youthfulness I was still attracted by the exotic aestheticism of the modern Russian pre-Raphaelite, Pavel Tchelitchew, whose tongue was even worse, although I knew that he was not a real painter. The portrait of me that Virgil had painted for Gertrude was, in her words, exotic. I have often been luxurious but very rarely exotic, as Gertrude and Alice soon found out. I like simple things, but they must be perfect and in character (as Gertrude Stein once pointed out), I am Scottish and Spanish and not English and French as many people think. That I am wildly passionate and do everything with fervour is true; that I romance I am willing to admit; but that I am unbalanced and weak is false. Gertrude used to say, when this accusation was made, or when friends became worried about one of my passions, "Don't worry, Francis will always come out with his head well screwed on to his shoulders. I think that any Scot, no matter how mixed his blood may be, will always have something shrewd and calculating about him."

Gertrude started asking many people to meet me, people I had not met with Cocteau or the surrealists. These people were mostly French or American: there were Bernard Fay, Louis Bromfield, Raymond Escholier, and Georges Maratier who all became friends and supporters of my work. And Elizabeth de Grammant, the Duchesse de Clermont-Tonnerre (who formed a group around Colette), Natalie Barney, who was a friend of Gertrude, and Alice and Marie Laurençin. Gertrude asked people to see my paintings, and she would explain to them and point things out that even I was not aware of. At afternoon receptions, Alice Toklas silently presided over the tea and cookies: she acted like a shadow behind Gertrude and was really the power behind the throne. It was she who always made the final decisions; whether it was concerning the dismissal of friends, such as in the case of Virgil Thomson, or their reinstatement, but her real devotion was for Gertrude Stein's mind and this almost amounted to adoration. Gertrude Stein wrote many things about painting which painters do not know or have forgotten. She said: "Everyone must love something: some people will love eating, some people will love drinking, some will love making money, while others love spending it; some will love the theatre, and some will even love sculptures, some will love gardening, some will love dogs, and some will really love painting."

I was invited to visit Bilignin with Bernard Fay, the great historian and Membre du Collège de France, who had written books in English on George Washington and

Benjamin Franklin. At the same time, Maria Cuttuli, the wife of a senator of Constantine in Algeria, who owned the Gallery Mybor in Paris, asked me to have my first exhibition on the first floor, at the same time as the ground floor was being used for an exhibition of the young Spaniard, Salvador Dali. Cocteau had shown me a painting by this young Spanish "miniaturist," who painted very carefully in glazes like a Flemish primitive —obviously very often done with a magnifying glass. He had been taken up by the surrealists. I accepted both invitations. Bilignin was the ancient gentleman's dwelling that Gertrude Stein had rented from a French army officer near the small town of Belley, where Brillat-Savarin had lived. Alive had found Pernotlet, a cook who had run a little hotel where the food had been the finest that could be found in France. They had seen Bilignin from across the valley at the spot from where I painted it amidst clouds of vicious gnats, who did not only bite me, but also got into my paints. It was a lovely old house with a mansard roof, a room frescoed with musical instruments, and a garden of box hedges. Alice Toklas, who was a great cook, liked the neighborhood —there was trout in the nearby lakes, *écrevisses* in the streams, and the best *quenelles* in the world, as well as a walled kitchen garden, where in the early morning she could pick the strawberries or other fruit "before the sun had kissed them." It was not only the country of Brillat-Savarin, but also of Madame Récamier and Châteaubriand. Baltus, the Swiss-English painter, who tried hard to keep portraiture alive, lived near the Benedictine monks of Hautecombe, where Bernard Fay went on retreats, which was on the Lac du Bourget facing Aix-les-Bains. It was superb for these two magnificently American and cultured ladies.

In the evenings at Bilignin, when I had finished painting for the day, Gertrude would tell me, as she rocked back and forth in her rocking-chair, nursing her dog, her opinion on all manner of subjects, in her deep quiet voice, which was one of the most beautiful that I have ever heard. Alice Toklas would be quietly tatting, at a large Picasso design, which she did not like (it had been given to her by Pablo as a present): he had sketched the design directly on to the material which was stretched on her frame. When it was almost finished, and while Alice was actually working on it, Pablo arrived on one of his visits and when he saw the exquisitely worked canvas he criticized one of the yellows Alice had used, unjustly as he had not indicated it properly. This upset Alice and made Gertrude furious. To add to this, he had arrived with someone who was not expected and a large Saluki hound who promptly "disturbed" Basket. The upshot of this was one of the famous "Gertrude and Pablo" rows, only this one lasted for two years and ended, according to Gertrude, in a Paris street where they met while she was walking her dog. Gertrude, when telling me about it later, said, "He was so sad, so unhappy, that I said to him, 'Pablo, what's this about—are you still writing bad poetry or painting serious pictures?' He was not angry but just Spanish, and said, '*Alors, ma Gertrude,*' so we kissed a great deal while a great many people looked at us." Many years later Alice gave her version of the story. They had moved into the rue Christine which is a tiny seventeenth-century street leading into the rue des Grands Augustins where Picasso had taken a superb palace for his working studio. Alice said that she and Gertrude met Pablo and Dora Maar, who was at the time his wife, by accident in the street and that Pablo had run across and greeted Gertrude with much affection leaving her to cope with Dora. Picasso and Gertrude walked ahead talking, Picasso in a very animated manner and Gertrude calmly dictating. Alice thought that they were heading for the Catalan restaurant which at that time was being partly run by Georges Hugnet and was decorated by his interesting collection of superb paintings by Miró, with surrealists and strange objects he had picked up in junk shops. Suddenly Picasso turned and addressed his wife, Dora Maar: "*C'est fini.*" And it really was, for it was a long time before they saw each other again. Gertrude said that it was because Picasso could not stand a woman painting and Dora had started painting. He is Spanish about women in his mind; they are there to have children, look after the house, and obey him. Dora Maar nearly died, but since then she has proved herself by becoming one of the best figurative painters of the day—her sense of landscape and colour have the quality of Turner. This was, of course, the end of another Pablo and Gertrude dispute.

The talks I had with Gertrude when she was rocking in her chair were mostly about painting, people, and herself. During one of my first visits to Bilignin, as I made many before I left for the East and when I came back, she was writing *The Autobiography of Alice B. Toklas,* as Alice never got down to writing it herself. Gertrude could only sleep in a room facing north without a view, and she worked most of the morning in bed. Later she came down when Alice had finished attending to the house and dogs, and would go into a tiny room where Alice typed on a kitchen table from Gertrude's notes which were always written in children's copybooks with pictures on the covers. Around the walls of their room were piles of detective books in bright paper bindings, as Gertrude read at least one a day. She did not like seeing books around the house, so they were hidden away in cupboards, and as she liked hoarding objects a place had to be found for everything from Chinese tea-pots to the crime series. It had always been Gertrude Stein's intention to write a detective story called *Blood on the Dining-Floor,* but death cheated her from ever achieving this game of words. She liked few books besides the *Old Elizabethans,* whom she resembled, and Richardson's *Clarissa.* The rest, especially after the Brontës, only interested her. Hard and determined as any Elizabethan adventurer, Gertrude Stein finally created an American language which was only based on English but not meant to be proper English. She had opened the eyes of young authors to the enjoyment of both.

Talking about herself, she told me that the first picture that she had liked was a painted panorama of the Battle of Waterloo which she had seen in Baltimore at the age of eight, but the subject did not interest her as much as the painting. Later she liked a picture of a man with a hoe, because she had lived mostly out of doors in the fresh air and this painting enthralled her as it was different from what she had observed. The first painting she bought was by Schilling, an American artist, because "it was a piece of American sky and American country." When she saw the Louvre she started liking museums, and she discovered that looking out of windows when the walls behind her were filled with pictures in gold frames stimulated her desire to look again at the painted surfaces. When she was tired from sight-seeing in Italy she found that it was pleasant to sleep on the plush benches in museums, as waking in front of a great picture, especially a Tintoretto, was most exciting. In Spain the treatment of white paint by the great masters fascinated her. "Why was white white, and Spanish too?" However Velázquez worried her, as she found his work too real to give pleasure. For a woman of her generation she made another important discovery in Spain, and that was El Greco. When she decided to live in Paris rather than in Spain, although her outlook changed, she regretted El Greco and St. Teresa's tiny garden in Avila.

Gertrude Stein liked to be familiar with paintings as well as with people and their settings. Her surroundings in Paris did not look like the paintings of the old masters as they had done in Spain. The things she saw in Paris were new, and this gave her a headache until one day, on one of her wanderings, she saw a picture shop with a landscape in the window that she liked and was familiar with. The dealer was Vollard, and the picture was by Cézanne, but after looking at a lot of paintings on many occasions by herself or with her brother Leo, she decided she liked Cézanne's figures best because they looked more like the people she saw than the trees and apples. She bought a group of bathers and a large portrait of his wife. It was the first portrait, she told me, that Cézanne had sold.

Gertrude Stein had a good old-fashioned eye for European paintings. I did not agree with her passion for oil paint on flat surfaces and a painting being limited to the canvas in a frame. The canvas is a magnet which draws the eye, not only into static composition, but to the centre from which all can emerge and be spread indefinitely or be drawn in to a heart which breathes. Today the problem of a painter is not the same as for Old Masters, who led their spectator by a highly studied route to the picture itself, but one that is closer to Chinese calligraphy, where the artist's interpretation of nature exists in the medium of his painting more than in the vision of any figurative sub-ject. A controlled palette of living textures leads the spectator to the meaning of the vitality of the work . . .

To return to the pleasant days I spent, as I have al-ready said many times, with Gertrude and Alice in the landscape country around Bilignin. Gertrude had also visited La Porte des Isles, and liked Mougins. Ger-trude's new Ford, which replaced the old Model T she had bought in the 'twenties, went fast, and Ger-trude drove fast, looking at things and pointing at them while Alice hung on to her hat. We had to visit every house, church, and interesting shop within miles and

I had to paint while Alice shopped. Gertrude was writing *Lucy Church Amiably*. Lucy was a village and the church had a Russian steeple which a soldier had brought back from the disastrous Napoleonic campaign. It was a hat, and the church became the woman, Lucy Church, in the book. I painted a straight landscape of this church while Gertrude watched me. I also painted the waterfall which is a person in the book too, though it was not at Lucy but several miles away. We visited Baltus and looked at his hard, solid figures full of brown which he painted against backgrounds of empty rooms with kitchen tables or bare sheets that reminded me of English mining towns. There was a wonderful portrait of children and a study for a fine portrait of the huge Dérain. I picked red and black currants in their garden whilst Alice Toklas carried a basket.

The only unhappy incident of my many visits to Bilignin occurred when I had stopped off to say goodbye to them before they left on Gertrude Stein's famous lecture tour of her native United States, which she had not seen for the thirty years and which delighted her as she saw her name for the first time in the headlines of the news in Times Square: "Gertrude Stein has arrived in New York." She loved it, she told me, especially as she was eating her first hamburger and it was salted. Gertrude had been forbidden to eat salt by her doctor for several years. The next day she discovered that flying was like looking at a cubist picture. The unhappy incident was a trivial row about a dog called Pépé which Francis Picabia had given Gertrude when she was visiting La Porte des Isles. Pépé was brother to my favourite little dog, The Squeak—a Mexican chihuahua. However, Gertrude took me to see her new discovery: it was a little landscape painted by a child on the walls of a ruined castle. And it was signed

Francis Rose. I do not know who had done it, but it seemed quite old. When I was leaving, Gertrude came to the door of my car and we hugged and kissed—I was not to see her again until 1938.

BRAVIG IMBS

Bravig Imbs was one of the pleasant young men who could be found among Gertrude Stein's admirers in the years between the wars. When he met her in 1926, his claim to artistic achievement was the publication of a novel, *The Professor's Wife*, a somewhat realistic portrayal of the wife of a Dartmouth teacher. The woman's disturbance at the characterization prompted Imbs to leave the college. He came to Paris, where he found sympathy and friendship from such artists as Pavel Tchelitchew (Pavlik, in the selection), his sister Choura, René Crevel, and Georges Maratier.

For the five years during which his friendship with Gertrude Stein flourished, he was devoted and reverent. As Virgil Thomson recalled, Imbs was "serviceable as an extra young man, good at errands, and pleasing in the home." To amuse Miss Stein, he would play her favorite tune, "The Trail of the Lonesome Pine," on the violin. But even more agreeable to her were his letters, full of admiration and compliments, acknowledging her encouragement. "You always remind me I am a person," he once wrote, "and then I feel better."

But this warm relationship, like so many others for Gertrude Stein, was short-lived. According to Thomson, a close member of the Stein circle at that time, Imbs had made the mistake of bringing his pregnant wife to a boarding house in Belley, near Miss Stein's country home. Gertrude Stein, whose aversion to childbirth apparently was well known to everyone but Imbs, looked with distaste at the prospect of seeing Valeska Imbs through her pregnancy. Alice Toklas, as usual, solved the problem by informing Bravig that the friendship was ended.

In 1944, more than a decade later, Imbs returned to Paris as a radio announcer, known throughout France as "Monsieur Bobby." Past difficulties forgotten, Stein greeted him warmly, but their friendship was rekindled only briefly; soon afterward Imbs was killed in an automobile crash.

❧ *Bravig Imbs* / *from* Confessions of Another Young Man

The day was Mardi Gras, and in some places on the Boulevards, people were courageously carrying on a Carnival; the weather was disagreeably damp and cold and the sky a sad, sad grey. I spent the best part of the afternoon shaving and washing and making sartorial preparations as though I were going to a ceremony.

I remember what difficulty I had selecting a tie and finally decided I had better dress as simply as possible, wearing a dark blue suit, white shirt, dark blue tie and handkerchief, dark blue socks, black shoes. But the combination seemed so sober and banal, I slipped a thin crystal bracelet . . . on my wrist, and then hastened off in a taxi to fetch Choura.

Choura was waiting for me calmly, pertly, wearing a stiff taffeta frock, and looking very pretty indeed with her brightly rouged lips. She really did have *le charme slav*. People turned to stare at her as we walked down the Boulevard Raspail.

Miss Stein's house, not far off, stood in a courtyard which always looked the same, summer and winter, paved in stone with an oval plot of evergreen plants in the center. I had become so panic-stricken by the time we reached the simple little door, with its window of ground glass, that I hastily slipped off the bracelet, feeling that it would be better to remain as simple as possible, and to say nothing.

In a moment, we had entered the bright little hall with its mirrors and umbrella vase and barometer and elaborate sconces, and I felt the servant's scrutiny as I took off my top coat. She was the famous Louise who had opened the door for Picasso, Matisse and Satie, and though she looked very stern and austere I was certain she liked me.

The entrance to the studio was by way of a very small painted grey door, and involuntarily one had to stoop, entering it. I remember the feeling of fatigue, mingled with my excitement, at the prospect of seeing this important room. I am like a cat in that I can't be happy in a place new to me until I know all the doors and windows, the good chairs and the shaky one, the tables and the bibelots—especially the easily breakable bibelots—and the pictures on the wall. As one cannot politely go sniffing around the moment one enters a room for the first time, all the observation has to be done surreptitiously, and this is tiring.

Gertrude Stein had no such feeling. She was always changing the room about to the infinite annoyance of her sculptor friend, Janet Scudder, and myself, who both felt that furniture and objects should stay put in one place, once and for all. I would just get accustomed to a new arrangement and could devote myself unreservedly to converstation, when Gertrude would switch the chairs about again, involving most delicate calculations on my part as to the effect the new groupings would have on the guests and intimate friends.

Gertrude received so many people that she could not be bothered worrying whether they would get on together, but let all classes and kinds mix pell-mell and the devil take the hindmost. All she cared about was to shake loose the people who bored or annoyed her and though she was too kindly to drop them in the middle of a sentence, she always managed to introduce them to Alice before the sentence was ended. Alice acted both as a sieve and buckler; she defended Gertrude from the bores and most of the new people were strained through her before Gertrude had any prolonged contact with them.

That was why after the preliminary handshaking, I found myself taking very delicious tea and munching heavenly cakes with the gypsy-like person I had noticed with Gertrude at the gallery. She talked a blue streak. Without fluttering, or losing the trend of thought, or saying anything superfluous, Alice Toklas could keep up a most intense, elaborate and rapid flow of conversation. If you really listened you very quickly fell under the mild hypnotic state which her mental pyrotechnics induced, and then, with her brown eyes slightly glittering, she would dart questions like arrows, and in three minutes, would know your place of birth, your environment, your family, your connections, your education, and your immediate intentions. And she never forgot what she acquired. I remember, years later, when conversation would come to a dead center and Gertrude seemed to have nothing to say, I had only to ask some questions about an American family in Paris, and Alice would spend the rest of the evening giving their history with most complete and fascinating detail.

Of course, I did not realize exactly what was happening to me as I heard Alice talking about Mardi Gras being so much gayer in the old days, for I was too busy snatching stares to the left and right of me. Every square inch in the room was interesting, but it was so very softly lit by low table lamps and four magnificent candles in ornate silver sticks that I was hard put to make out certain objects, and the lovely blue Picassos, high on one wall, were all but invisible. Nevertheless, I was able to appreciate the perfect arrangement of the paintings—there must have been nearly a hundred of them—all hung close together and literally covering the walls. And yet no picture impinged on another, and each seemed in its proper place. There was no sensation of being in a museum either—the room had a distinctive life all its own—and that was, I suppose, due to the fact that each picture had its peculiar merit.

"Visiting Miss Stein is like visiting a school," the Chilean painter, Guevara, said once to me, "she has an example of every phase and period of modern painting and generally the best one."

Of course, there was nothing sacrosanct about the arrangement of the pictures. Like the chairs, Gertrude shifted them about a good deal, and the Tchelit-chews made way for the Tonnys and the Tonnys for the Francis Roses, but whichever way she shifted them seemed right. She did not lose herself in conjecture and experiment while doing this, as I would have done, but merely adopted certain pictures as pivots and grouped the other paintings about them. It was Elliot Paul who pointed out this procedure to me, simply because he was so fond of the chief pivot picture, the famed Picasso: a nude of a young girl, bearing a basket of flowers. It was one of the few paintings that Picasso had ever used a model for, and Gertrude so liked it when she first saw it that she bought it for a hundred gold francs. For my part, I preferred the nude that complemented it on the other side of the fireplace—tawny and Asiatic and darkly rose.

I had very little time that day, however, to look at the paintings the way I longed to, for I realized instinctively that Alice was important and required attention. My one idea, having arrived, was to be invited again, not out of any snobbishness, but because I knew Gertrude Stein could teach me a great deal about writing. So I nodded and yessed and noed while Alice Toklas talked on and on, and kept one ear strained to hear the conversation between Choura and Miss Stein.

Choura, genial, explosive, good humored, was recounting the departure of Allen and Pavlik for Tunis; how Pavlik had insisted on taking his easel and paints and brushes and canvases, so that he looked like Tartarin preparing for a lion hunt, and how Allen disappeared at the last minute to say good-bye to the grocer and give a farewell kiss to the girl at the creamery.

Gertrude began to laugh. She had the easiest, most engaging and infectious laugh I have ever heard. Always starting abruptly at a high pitch and cascading down and down into rolls and rolls of unctuous merriment, her hearty laugh would fill the room and then, as it gradually dwindled into chuckles and appreciative murmurs, the silence that followed seemed golden with sunlight. Her laugh was boisterous but I have never known it to offend even the most delicately attuned, for it was so straight from the heart, so human, so rich in sound.

I was startled when I first heard it that day, for like Sherwood Anderson, I, too, had foolishly expected a woman inscrutable and mysterious, and not this vital, headstrong and cordial personality. I was at once disappointed and relieved that such was the case, for though I was young enough to bear the divine heights more than five minutes at a time, it was much more agreeable to have to do with a human person.

Gertrude was very pleasant to me that day (for Alice finally let me go to her) but as she told me afterwards, judging from Pavlik's letter she thought I must be just another YMCA secretary and she had seen so many in the War that she never wanted to see any more of them. But, as she explained later to me, she had become puzzled at my answers which were not the answers she had expected, and to get this matter straight, to have me placed to her satisfaction, she decided on the spot to invite me again. When I heard her ask me to return, I was overjoyed and left with Choura, shortly after, treading on air.

Degrees of intimacy were very carefully graded in the

Stein household and one was made to feel them keenly, so that when the first important degree was reached, that of being invited to lunch, one was all but overcome by this honor.

The supreme degree, of course, was a quarrel, and Allen, who had lunched and dined there and been invited to the Ain, and been sat with many, many times, was already planning for it.

"She's the greatest artist in the world," he said, "but, my dear, she has such a temper, such a temper! She has already had three violent quarrels with Picasso and I suppose ours is coming along." He pretended to be resigned to the event but I could see that he did not find the prospect too unpleasant. I suppose that was the Irish in him.

At any rate, both Pavlik and Allen were very careful not to let me go alone to Gertrude's, for they held the balance of power in the salon and did not want it to be jeopardized. I had no such intention in mind, for I could not be attracted by the particular glory of such procedure, and, on the contrary, I was very glad that they chose to accompany me, for I had not completely recovered from my initial fright of Gertrude. Pavlik was delighted that I had found someone who inspired me with awe, for almost all the time I was with him, he was lecturing me, telling how insufferably young I was, how disagreeably persistent, how fundamentally vain and stupid. He recounted with malicious glee that Gertrude was not at all sure of me, and that she had found me *"rose dans tous les sens."*

Pavlik was painting my portrait then. He intended to paint three, the third to be mine, but after he had finished the first two he said it made him sick to look at my face any more and refused to continue. He was in a bad period at the time, and neither of the two portraits was any good. I was very disappointed, of course, and very depressed at all his scolding, but it had the effect of making me start work. I had to justify myself and so started writing some short stories.

I showed them to Gertrude, and she, with unerring accuracy, was able to point out the phrases, sentences and paragraphs where the literary intuition had been direct and pure, as well as those parts where substitution for the intuition had been made.

"You have the gift of true brilliancy," she said to me, "and less than anyone should you use crutch phrases. Either the phrase must come or it must not be written at all. I have never understood how people could labor over a manuscript, write and rewrite it many times, for to me, if you have something to say, the words are always there. And they are the exact words and the words that should be used. If the story does not come whole, *tant pis,* it has been spoiled, and that is the most difficult thing in writing, to be true enough to yourself, and to know yourself enough so that there is no obstacle to the story's coming through complete. You see how you have faltered, and halted, and fallen down in your story, all because you have not solved this problem of communication for yourself. It is the fundamental problem in writing and has nothing to do with métier, or with sentence building, or with rhythm. In my own writing, as you know, I have destroyed sentences and rhythms and literary overtones and all the rest of that nonsense, to get to the very core of this problem of the communication of the intuition. If the communication is perfect, the words have life, and that is all there is to good writing, putting down on the paper words which dance and weep and make love and fight and kiss and perform miracles."

Gertrude had the secret of imparting enthusiasm to others, for as an artist, she was sincere and she felt deeply and she was bound up in her own writing, an humble subject in the kingdom of words. She rarely indulged in such outbursts, but generally marked with a faint pencil across the sentences or words which displeased her in my manuscripts and it was up to me to find out why they were wrong. When she did have something important to say, she said it rapidly, monotonously, almost with embarrassment; she much preferred to talk about baseball or the American doughboys or gardens or the cuisine of the Ain. It was then she could laugh and expand and radiate; writing for her meant discipline and duty and loyalties, all those elements in life which restrict and hamper.

"The words must be serried if the style is to be good," she would say with a great deal of seriousness.

It was at such moments that Gertrude looked very like a monk, austere, illuminated, grave—the look monks have on their faces when they are officiating— and I remember the impression was even more striking after she had had her hair cut short. Pavlik almost went out of his mind for an afternoon on account of that incident. He had a very easy classification of women: either they looked like his mother, his dear aunt or his sister. Gertrude had always looked like the dear aunt, and now with her topknot shorn away she did not look like anyone but herself—and Pavlik did not know where to place her. He had been planning for months to make her portrait, too—although always scared to death of the Picasso portrait which stared gloomily at him from the wall as if to say, just try to do better than I!—and now the shape of her head seemed quite changed and all his problems sprang up anew with fresh thorns. Of course, Pavlik was too polite to say what he really thought, but I think he could have choked Alice with pleasure for having played the barber.

It was at the beginning of the year and Gertrude simply felt she ought to make a change of some kind; Alice suggested cutting her hair as a way of passing that Sunday afternoon, and I must say she did it very well. Gertrude looked much more handsome, because her former coiffure had seemed somewhat Victorian, and this coiffure was at least modern.

Pavlik immediately went off the deep end when he saw her and then when he realized that Gertrude really wanted him to like it he composed himself enough to say that it really didn't make any difference. He never painted her portrait though he painted Alice's, as a kind of preparatory exercise. That painting was long and narrow and all in dull dark blues; it gave Alice a sleepy vulture look which was very strange.

Alice liked it but Gertrude did not, and Pavlik got out of that situation by telling all his friends that Gertrude liked it but that Alice loathed it, loathed him, and set up such antagonistic vibrations that it would be impossible for him to paint Gertrude's portrait. It was not exactly that Pavlik had cold feet, but he was a Russian to the core, and it did distress him that he should be kowtowing to a Jewess.

Whenever that subject came up, Allen would unctuously pour oil on the troubled waters and say: "Gertrude is the most un-Jewish person I ever knew. She is so dangerous and tolerant and has such a magnificent brain. Those aren't Jewish traits." Pavlik would struggle a while and then would cede, saying, "Yes, yes, Gertrude is magnificent, she knows so much about painting, she has such perfect taste and yet she can't draw a cow. That's wonderful."

As a matter of fact, I don't think Gertrude knew much about paintings at any time. Her flair was for people and particularly for genius and she seldom erred. Her capacity for sizing up a person's character in a relatively brief time was of an uncanny precision—although Gertrude had nothing of the occult about her. She was always much more interested in the painter than in what he was doing and she measured his artistic worth by the amount of his resistance to her. She really had a great love for Picasso. "When he was young," she told me once, "his black eyes would flash white fire" —but Picasso was as hard as nails and had a Spaniard's attitude towards women and never, never yielded. Gertrude was attracted to his genius, for it was so akin to her own, a Phoenix-like genius capable of incredible destruction and incredible invention, but when the exchange between them was not perfectly balanced there would be those violent outbursts of temper and subsequent separations.

To avenge herself, Gertrude would buy more Picassos and sell her Matisses. She finally sold all the Matisses she had, except a drawing of some flowers in a goblet, a most exquisite drawing which hung in her dining room and which I often coveted. Of course, it was Alice who was anti-Matisse, and whenever Gertrude was in the mood for selling she would urge her to dispose of the Matisses.

"He never knew what size canvas to use," Alice would say to me with proper distaste.

I think Alice had a much surer feeling for painting than Gertrude, but very few people knew that, for it was always Gertrude who had the word in public. I remember the way they would barge down the rue de la Boétie in Godiva—that utterly charming wreck of a Ford which was about to be classed as a historical monument along with the taxis of the Marne, when it was affectionately relegated to a comfortable shed in Créteil—Gertrude driving with a stern expression and Alice sitting beside her, elegant and detached, as though she were in a victoria, on their way to an exhibition. They were always going to exhibitions (and there were new exhibitions in Paris every day) in their search for new human beings. Of course, it was very rarely that they found any painting that interested them sufficiently to seek acquaintance with the artist, and more often than not, the most interesting artists would make their way by themselves to the rue de Fleurus.

Gertrude's prestige was enormous, for she had undoubtedly been the only person in Paris to have faith in Picasso's sanity when he began Cubism. She bought the first two Cubist paintings Picasso created, pictures of a Spanish village, and everyone thought she had lost her mind. She continued adding to her collection, and Picasso sold her the best, for he was touched by her confidence. Years later, when the merchants began falling all over themselves to buy Cubist paintings, they saw the error of their ways and began to have a holy respect for Gertrude's opinions. She became an unofficial pontiff and the merchants dreaded her visits, for she could make or mar an exhibition with little more than a movement of her thumb. If she approved of an exhibition, she naturally carried off the best painting of the lot at a bargain price; if she disapproved, there was a whole coterie of American buyers who would follow her hint.

And so Gertrude's prestige as a modern art expert grew and grew, and all from the acorn of those two little Cubist paintings which she had purchased because she recognized Picasso's genius.

JOHN GLASSCO

At eighteen John Glassco left McGill University, where he was in his third year, to devote himself to composing Surrealist poetry. At first he shared an apartment in Montreal with his friend Graeme Taylor, who was intent on writing the great Canadian novel. "We were united by comradeship, a despisal of everything represented by the business world, the city of Montreal and the Canadian scene, and a desire to get away," Glassco wrote later. And it was to Paris that the two young men dreamed of going.

Though his father wanted him to be a lawyer and his mother saw him as a future bishop, Glassco maintained his independence and refused to return to college. "My real problem was a combination of precocity, impatience, and inability to take in anything from books. I already existed in a climate of restlessness, scorn, frequent ecstasy and occasional despair."

Determined to be a poet, and bent on experiencing bohemian life in Paris, Glassco and his friend managed to obtain passage on a government cargo ship; in 1928 they were sharing a room on the quiet rue Broca, ready to find "the dream of excellence and beauty" which they hoped awaited them.

It did not take long for Glassco to abandon Surrealist poetry and turn, instead, to writing his memoirs, à la George Moore. But even this task was tempered by his sudden discovery that "literature isn't so important as life." "For the first time I can feel the movement of my thoughts, the pulse of my youth," he wrote. "I had only to think I was now in the city of Baudelaire, Utrillo and Apollinaire to be swept by a joy so strong it verged on nausea."

He and Graeme Taylor soon penetrated the literary circles of Montparnasse. The slender, blond Canadian, called Buffy by his friends, reminded some of the ethereal Nijinsky. Though he was younger than most of the writers he was meeting, he struck them as mature and already somewhat disillusioned. He could be found often in the company of Robert McAlmon; from the first, Glassco had been "impressed by his charm, loneliness and bitterness, touched by his vanity and refreshed by his rudeness." Through McAlmon he was introduced to a compatriot, novelist Morley Callaghan. From time to time their circle was enlivened by the photographer and Surrealist painter Narwhal, a humorous figure, "tall and thin, with large horn-rimmed glasses and a talon-shaped nose like an owl's."

It was through the persuasion of Graeme Taylor's girl friend, Caridad, that Glassco arrived at Gertrude Stein's studio during one of her gatherings. McAlmon refused to accompany the three to "lap up the literary vomit."

Glassco's impressions of Gertrude Stein were recorded four years later in the Royal Victoria Hospital in Montreal, where he was being treated for tuberculosis. His reminiscences, *Memoirs of Montparnasse,* were written "to record, and in a sense re-live, a period of great happiness." The book was followed by two volumes of his own verse, and an edition of French-Canadian poetry.

🌿 John Glassco / from Memoirs of
Montparnasse

"Now," said Caridad, pouring a ten-cent rum into her coffee, "we shall go soon to Miss Gertrude Stein's and absorb an international culture. Her parties are very well behaved and there are always plenty of rich men—which I find very agreeable. A girl must live. Bob,* you must show yourself there—you, celebrated man of letters, publisher, man of the world. It will also make my own entrance so much more impressive—with three cavaliers. Come, it is only a few streets away—"

"Rats, I know the place. I've been to her parties. Never again. Gertrude paid me to publish her lousy five-pound book and we've never been the same since. She thinks I held back some of the proceeds. No, you three run along."

Although neither Graeme nor I cared for Gertrude Stein's work, we really wanted to see the great woman. I was thinking too of how I would write my father about meeting her, and that (once he had checked her credentials with the English Department at McGill) he might just raise my allowance. The business of living on fifty dollars a month was becoming almost impossible; we were always short of money, we were never able to eat or drink enough, and while Bob was often generous it was apparent his own resources were running low and he would soon have to make another requisition on his father-in-law. As foreigners we could take no regular

*Robert McAlmon.

work, and while Graeme's skill with the poker dice seldom failed, it often took him over an hour to win 100 francs and obliged him to endure as well the conversation of the dreariest types of American barfly; the worst of it was that he had to spend almost a quarter of his winnings drinking with them during his operations.

Accordingly, we set off with Caridad down the boulevard Raspail in the plum-blue light of the June evening, arrived at the rue de Fleurus, and were greeted at the door by a deciduous female who seemed startled by the sight of Caridad.

"Miss Toklas!" Caridad cried affectionately. "It is so long since we have not met. I am Caridad de Plumas, you will remember, and these are my two young Canadian squires to whom I wish to give the privilege of meeting you and your famous friend. We were coming with Mr. Robert McAlmon, but he is unavoidably detained.

As she delivered this speech she floated irresistibly forward, Miss Toklas retreated, and we found ourselves in a big room already filled with soberly dressed and soft-spoken people.

The atmosphere was almost ecclesiastical and I was glad to be wearing my best dark suit, which I had put on to meet Morley Callaghan. I had begun to suspect that Caridad had not been invited to the party and all of us were in fact crashing the gate. But Caridad, whether invited or not, was in a few minutes a shining centre of the party: her dyed hair caught the subdued light. She paid no further attention to Graeme or myself, and I understood that she was as usual looking for rich men.

The room was large and sombrely furnished, but the walls held, crushed together, a magnificent collection of paintings—Braques, Matisses, Picassos, and Picabias. I only recovered from their cumulative effect to fall under that of their owner, who was presiding like a Buddha at the far end of the room.

Gertrude Stein projected a remarkable power, possibly due to the atmosphere of adulation that surrounded her. A rhomboidal woman dressed in a floor-length gown apparently made of some kind of burlap, she gave the impression of absolute irrefragability; her ankles, almost concealed by the hieratic folds of her dress, were like the pillars of a temple: it was impossible to conceive of her lying down. Her fine close-cropped head was in the style of the late Roman Empire, but unfortunately it merged into broad peasant shoulders without the aesthetic assistance of a neck; her eyes were large and much too piercing. I had a peculiar sense of mingled attraction and repulsion towards her. She awakened in me a feeling of instinctive hostility coupled with a grudging veneration, as if she were a pagan idol in whom I was unable to believe.

Her eyes took me in, dismissed me as someone she did not know, and returned to her own little circle. With a feeling of discomfort I decided to find Graeme and disappear: this party, I knew, was not for me. But just then Narwhal came up and began talking so amusingly that I could not drag myself away.

"I have been reading the works of Jane Austen for the first time," he said in his quiet nasal voice, "and I'm looking for someone to share my enthusiasm. Now these are very good novels in my opinion. You wouldn't believe it but here—among all these writers, people who are presumably literary ahtists—I can't find anyone who has read her books with any real attention. In fact most of them don't seem to like her work at all. But I find this dislike is founded on a false impression that she was a respectable woman."

"Jane Austen?"

"I don't mean to say she was loose in her behavior, or not a veuhjin. I'm sure she was a veuhjin. I mean she was aristocratic, not bourgeoise, she was no creep, she didn't really give a darn about all those conventions of chaystity and decorum."

"Well, her heroines did."

"Oh sure, they *seem* to, they've got to, or else there'd be no story. But Austen didn't herself. Who is the heroine, the Ur-heroine of *Sense and Sensibility?* It's Marianne, not Elinor. Of *Pride and Prejudice?* It's the girl that runs off with the military man. What's wrong with *Emma?* Emma."

"You mean Willoughby and Wickham are her real heroes?"

"No, they're just stooges, see? But they represent the dark life-principle of action and virility that Austen really admired, like Marianne and Lydia stand for the life force of female letting-go. And when Ann Elliott falls for Captain Wentworth—you'll notice he's the third W of the lot—it's the same thing, only this time he's tamed. It's a new conception of Austen's talent which I formed yesterday, and which was suggested to me by the fact that Prince Lucifer is the real hero of *Paradise Lost,* as all the savants declare."

This idea of Jane Austen as a kind of early D. H. Lawrence was new. Never had the value of her books been so confirmed as by this extraordinary interpretation of them: it was a real tribute.

"Do you happen to know if there were any portraits of Austen made?" he asked.

"A water colour by a cousin, I think."

"Good! I guess it's lousy then," he said with satisfaction. "Because I've been thinking of doing an imaginary portrait of her too. I see her in a wood, in a long white dress. She's looking at a mushroom. But all around her are these thick young trees growing straight up—some are black with little white collars and stand for ministers of the church and some are blue and stand for officers in the Royal English Navy. I'm also thinking of putting some miniature people, kind of elves dressed like witches and so forth, in the background—but I'm not sure."

"It sounds good."

"The focus of the whole thing will be the mushroom," he said. "It represents the almost overnight flowering of her genius—also its circumscribed quality, its suggestion of being both sheltered *and* a shelter—see?— and its e-conomy of structure."

"An edible mushroom?"

"You've got it. That will be the whole mystery of the portrait. The viewer won't know and she won't know either. We will all partake of Jane Austen's doubt, faced with the appalling mystery of sex."

We must have been talking with an animation unusual for one of Gertrude Stein's parties, for several of the guests had already gathered around us.

"You are talking of Jane Austen and sex, gentlemen?" said a tweedy Englishman with a long ginger moustache. "The subjects are mutually exclusive. That dired-up lady snob lived behind lace curtains all her life. She's of no more importance than a chromo. Isn't that so, Gertrude?"

I was suddenly aware that our hostess had advanced and was looking at me with her piercing eyes.

"Do I know you?" she said. "No. I suppose you are just one of those silly young men who admire Jane Austen."

Narwhal had quietly disappeared and I was faced by Miss Stein, the tweedy man and Miss Toklas. Already uncomfortable at being an uninvited guest, I found the calculated insolence of her tone intolerable and lost my temper.

"Yes, I am," I said. "And I suppose you are just one of those silly old women who don't."

The fat Buddha-like face did not move. Miss Stein merely turned, like a gun revolving on its turret, and moved imperturbably away.

The tweedy man did not follow her. Leaning towards me, his moustache bristling, he said quietly, "If you don't leave here this moment, I will take great pleasure in throwing you out, bodily."

"If you really want," I said, "I'll wait outside in the street for three minutes, when I'll be glad to pull your nose."

I then made my exit, and after standing outside in the street for exactly three minutes on the sidewalk (by which time I was delighted to find he did not appear), I took my walk back to the Dôme. Graeme joined me there fifteen minutes later.

"That's the last party we go to without being invited," he said.

SAMUEL PUTNAM

Growing up in the plains of central Illinois, Samuel Putnam longed for faraway places and the sound of a foreign tongue. He felt an intuitive dislike for what Gertrude Stein called America's "loud-voiced, good-looking prosperity," for its chauvinism and provincialism. Throughout his boyhood he was aware of a growing need to escape the "smug Americanism" of his home town.

Finally, college offered liberation. At the University of Chicago Putnam reveled in the "spirit of free and untrammeled inquiry" which was prevalent among professors who dared to introduce to their students the writing of such "unorthodox" artists as Bernard Shaw, and among students left free to discover thinkers like Karl Marx.

After college Putnam went to work for the *Chicago Evening Post,* writing on art and literature. He found himself in the midst of the Chicago "renaissance" in those years when the city was the home of Margaret Anderson's *Little Review,* Harriet Monroe's *Poetry,* Carl Sandburg's *Day Book.* But the veneer of excitement soon wore thin for Putnam. Beneath the guise of liberation, behind a façade of modernity, he perceived the cold manipulation of poets by editors, the pontifical policies formulated by those already established in literature. He saw talented young poets rejected and destroyed.

Disillusioned and outspoken, he was urged by H. L. Mencken to write an article debunking "the phonies." "Chicago: An Obituary" was published in Mencken's *Mercury* in August 1926. The uproar it caused reverberated throughout the city.

Shortly afterward Putnam gave up newspaper work to devote himself to translating, a task he much preferred. He had already spent years on a modern translation of Rabelais; now he needed some time in France for study and research to complete the work. With assurances of financial assistance from publisher Pascal Covici, Putnam sailed to Europe with his wife and baby, third class on the shaky *Rochambeau*.

Paris, he found, was "nothing less than another world" from what he had known. "One may walk in rain and misery and still be comforted if not happy. . . ." He shared the Dôme and the Select with Ford Madox Ford, Hemingway, Ezra Pound, and Eugene and Maria Jolas, editors of *transition*.

One of his most frequent companions was Wambly Bald, whose column "Vie de Boheme" appeared in the Paris edition of the *Chicago Tribune*. Bald gathered his material by wandering around the Latin Quarter "like a slightly alcoholic ghost, seeing nothing, hearing nothing, and telling all." Their visit to Gertrude Stein is recorded in Putnam's *Paris Was Our Mistress,* the story of a generation in exile in a city "full of life and zest and color, as well as weariness, disillusionment, and despair. . . . The Paris that was our spiritual mistress, a wise and beautiful one, at a time when our own America, or so it seemed, had turned strumpet."

🌱 *Samuel Putnam / from* Paris Was
Our Mistress

Gertrude Stein lived in the rue de Fleurus, "about ten jumps from the Dôme," as my friend Wambly Bald put it; but the jumps would have had to be powerful ones. So far as her place of abode was concerned, she was not far removed from the roaring center of Montparnasse life; but for most residents of the Quarter she might as well have lived in Timbuktu.

Her topographical situation was typical of her attitude toward the outside world in general. She was remote and yet not remote. The common impression was that, like Joyce, she was a cloistered being, fearful of any intrusion; she was pictured as one who could be approached only with genuflections and the odor of incense; whereas the truth is that, unlike the creator of *Ulysses,* she was quite accessible to her admirers and to many of the press who chose to look in at her "studio" (there were not many that did in those days).

Miss Stein's acquaintance with Americans at this period seemed to be limited to Bravig Imbs, Elliot Paul, Glenway Wescott, Eugene Jolas and his wife Maria, and one or two others. Paul, upon Jolas's suggestion, had asked her to write for *transition,* and, according to Maria Jolas's statement, she had consented with sufficient alacrity. The magazine proceeded to reprint her *Tender Buttons* and in addition published her *Four Saints* opera and a bibliography of her work. Just what was the cause of the final break between *transition* and Miss Stein will perhaps never be told in print by those in a position to know; but the rupture was signalized by the publication of the *Autobiography of Alice B. Toklas* on the one hand and, on the other hand, by a blast in answer to this work, published in the form of a pamphlet, "Testimony Against Gertrude Stein," bearing the signatures of the Jolases, Matisse, Braque, André Salmon, and Tristan Tzara.

All this, however, was in the future. At the time of which I am speaking, Stein and Joyce were the two big thrills that *transition* had to offer its transatlantic customers; and pilgrims would come from afar—from as far away as Chicago and California—on the chance of being able to have a word with the author of *Tender Buttons* or the genius who was then engaged in producing the "Work in Progress." It may seem strange, but I think that more of them came to the rue de Fleurus than to Joyce's place, and it is also my impression that there were more women than men among Stein's devotees. What moral there is to this, I am sure I do not know; but if one is to judge from the reports brought back, she appeared to get on better with the women.

There was the case of Annie, the little girl who had read *Geography and Plays* and who had journeyed from Chicago to Paris because she simply must discuss the work with the author. Daughter of middle-class parents who had reared her to believe that her virginity was her jewel, Annie was a very beautiful young woman who, as she put it (for she was inclined to mysticism) "gave off vibrations." Give them off she certainly did; and what is more, she drove all the males nearly crazy as she sat at the Dôme by the hour and weightily pondered the question, seeking the advice of all present: "Should I or should I not lose my virginity?" Annie's first visit to the rue de Fleurus had been a great success and she had become a frequent visitor. One day she came back and announced that the question was settled.

Miss Stein had solved the problem for her. The solution? According to Annie, Miss Stein had said:

"To be a virgin is to be a virgin and not to be a virgin is not to be a virgin and not to be a virgin may be to be a virgin."

That, at any rate, was what Annie told us. I cannot vouch for it.

For my own part, I was always afraid of Gertrude. She reminded me a trifle too much of the cigar-smoking Amy Lowell, whom I had known in my younger days. Wambly Bald had named her "the Woman with a Face Like Caesar's," and it seemed to fit.

We were at the Dôme one afternoon when Wambly said: "Come on, let's go up and see Gertie."

"What do you mean? She'd throw us out."

Leo Stein, Gertrude's brother, was sitting with us.

"What are you afraid of?" he asked. "My God, Sam, you have no idea how dumb she is! Why, when we were in school, I used to have to do all her homework for her."

Leo and Gertrude definitely did not care for each other; and this remark, I reflected, must be a bit of exaggeration in view of his sister's record at Johns Hopkins and at Harvard in such abstruse subjects as brain anatomy and abnormal pathology. But it heartened me, nonetheless. I decided to go with Wambly.

"You do the talking," I said to him. "I'll stay in the background."

"And to think," he observed as we came up to the building in which Miss Stein lived, "and to think that it is from here that she has been saving the English language for the last twenty-five years!"

Inside, we found the walls covered with Picassos. Picasso, Picasso, Picasso, and more Picasso.

"Yes," Miss Stein informed us, "Picasso has done eighty portraits of me. I sat for that one ninety-one times."

Good newspaperman that he is, Wambly lost no time in coming to the point; and the interviewing technique that he chose to adopt, a belligerent one, proved to be admirably suited to the purpose of drawing out the interviewee. But still, I was mildly alarmed at his beginning.

"Your prose, Miss Stein," he blurted out, "strikes me as being obscure, deliberately obscure."

The Woman with the Face Like Caesar's never looked more like him than then, as she drew herself up haughtily and replied:

"My prose is obscure only to the lazy-minded. It is a well, a deep well, well it is like a well and that is well."

"There are some people," persisted Wambly, "who are inclined to believe that it is a bottomless well—or one with a false bottom."

At this, Miss Stein's eyes flashed like Caesar's on the field of battle and her voice rang as she answered:

"Naturally, I have my detractors. What genius does not?"

"You *are* a genius, then?" It was my first question. Miss Stein looked at me as if I were a dot that had suddenly appeared upon the map.

"There are three of us," she enunciated: "Myself, Picasso, and Whitehead." (She was to repeat this statement in her *Autobiography*.)

"What about Joyce?"

"Joyce," she admitted, "is *good*." (The italics were in her voice.) "He is a *good* writer. People like him because he is incomprehensible and anybody can understand him. But who came first, Gertrude Stein or James Joyce? Do not forget that my first great book, *Three Lives*, was published in 1908. That was long before *Ulysses*. But Joyce *has* done *something*. His influence, however, is local. Like Synge, another Irish writer, he has had his day. Won't you have some more tea?"

"You feel, then, Miss Stein, that your place in literature is secure?"

"My place in literature? Twentieth-century literature *is* Gertrude Stein. There was Henry James, of course—"

"Yes, there was Henry James—"

"He was my precursor, you might say; but everything really begins with my *Three Lives*."

At this point, Wambly saw fit to remind our hostess of something which Wyndham Lewis had just said about her. Lewis had implied that she was in the same class with Anita Loos.

"That," exclaimed Miss Stein, "is simply British propaganda—against great American writers! I am surprised that you pay any attention to it."

"You think that the English are jealous of the Americans?"

"They have a right to be. After all, America made the twentieth century just as England made the nineteenth. America has given Europe everything. America has given Europe Gertrude Stein—"

"What about the other great American writers?"

"There are the big four: Poe, Whitman, James, myself. The line of descent is clear. And James, Whitman, and Poe are dead. I am the last. But I am truly international. My reputation is growing all the time."

"Do you feel that your writing is really American, that is to say, typically American?"

"Certainly. What has been the tendency of American writing?"

Wambly and I exchanged glances, each waiting for the other to speak up.

"Toward abstraction, of course. But an abstraction without mysticism. That is the great contribution of Gertrude Stein. Her work is abstract without being mystical. There is no mysticism in my work."

"No mysticism?"

"None whatever," was the emphatic response. "My

work is perfectly natural. It is so natural that it is unnatural to those to whom the unnatural is natural. I reproduce things exactly as they are and that is all there is to it. The outer world becomes the inner world and the inner world becomes the outer, and the outward is no longer outward but inward and the inward is no longer inward but outward and it takes genius to do that and Gertrude Stein *is* a genius."

THORNTON WILDER

Thornton Wilder had visited Paris in the 1920s, often stopping in at Shakespeare and Company, where he seemed to Sylvia Beach "rather shy and a little like a young curate." But he met Gertrude Stein nearly a decade later, on the other side of the Atlantic, when he was a lecturer in comparative literature at the University of Chicago, where she had come to speak.

In Thornton Wilder, Stein found an advocate whose response to her work was both instinctive and unsentimental. She immediately recognized his "serious beliefs and precision," and her confidence in his opinions never diminished throughout their friendship. They spoke the common language of writers troubled by the same problems. "The conceptions of Human Nature and the Human Mind . . . the relations of Masterpieces to their apparent subject-matter. Those things . . . and identity," Wilder admitted, had "become cell and marrow in me. . . ."

These were the subjects of her lectures in Chicago, the problems she explored in *The Geographical History of America* and "What Are Masterpieces and Why Are There So Few of Them?," the questions they discussed when Wilder visited Stein in Paris and at her country home in Bilignin.

Wilder read Stein's work through the eyes of a scholar and wrote of them as one of America's most lauded artists. By the time he met Stein he had received the Pulitzer Prize for *The Bridge of San Luis Rey;* during the years he knew her he was awarded the prize twice again, for *Our Town* in 1938, for *The Skin Of Our Teeth* in 1943. Still, he thought himself "not an innovator but a rediscoverer of forgotten goods and I hope a remover of obtrusive bric-à-brac." Like Stein, he found ideas "in the great works of the past."

His belief in her work insured her place in American literature and lessened the impact of the derision she suffered by so many. She was, Wilder felt, one of those rare minds who "can . . . report life without adulterating the report with the gratifying movements of their own self-assertion, their private quarrel with what it has been to be a human being."

He saw in her "an impassioned listener to life," just as he had always been. "Neither her company nor her books were for those who have grown tired of listening," he wrote. "It was an irony that she did her work in a world in which for many reasons and for many appalling reasons people have so tired."

Four in America

Miss Gertrude Stein, answering a qeustion about her line

>   A rose is a rose is a rose is a rose,

once said with characteristic vehemence:

"Now listen! I'm no fool. I know that in daily life we don't say 'is a . . . is a . . . is a . . .' "

She knew that she was a difficult and an idiosyncratic author. She pursued her aims, however, with such conviction and intensity that occasionally she forgot that the results could be difficult to others. At such times the achievements she had made in writing, in "telling what she knew" (her most frequent formulization of the aim of writing) had to her the character of self-evident beauty and clarity. A friend, to whom she showed recently complete examples of her poetry, was frenquently driven to reply sadly: "But you forget that I don't understand examples of your extremer styles." To this she would reply with a mixture of bewilderment, distress, and exasperation:

"But what's the difficulty? Just read the words on the paper. They're in English. Just read them. Be simple and you'll understand these things."

Now let me quote the whole speech from which the opening remark . . . has been extracted. A student in her seminar at the University of Chicago had asked her for an "explanation" of the famous line. She leaned forward, giving all of herself to the questioner in that unforgettable way which has endeared her to hundreds of students and to hundreds of soldiers in two wars, trenchant, humorous, but above all urgently concerned over the enlightenment of even the most obtuse questioner:

"Now listen! Can't you see that when the language was new—as it was with Chaucer and Homer—the poet could use the name of a thing and the thing was really there? He could say 'O moon,' 'O sea,' 'O love' and the moon and the sea and love were really there. And can't you see that after hundreds of years had gone by and thousands of poems had been written, he could call on those words and find that they were just worn-out literary words? The excitingness of pure being had withdrawn from them; they were just rather stale literary words. Now the poet has to work in the excitingness of pure being; he has to get back that intensity into the language. We all know that it's hard to write poetry in a late age; and we know that you have to put some strangeness, something unexpected, into the structure of the sentence in order to bring back vitality to the noun. Now it's not enough to be bizarre; the strangeness in the sentence structure has to come from the poetic gift, too. That's why it's doubly hard to be a poet in a late age. Now you all have seen hundreds of poems about roses and you know in your bones that the rose is not these. All those songs that sopranos sing as encores about 'I have a garden; oh, what a garden!' Now I don't want to put too much emphasis on that line, because it's just one line in a longer poem. But I notice that you all know it; you make fun of it, but you know it. Now listen! I'm no fool. I know that in daily life we don't go around saying 'is a . . . is a . . . is a . . .' Yes, I'm no fool; but I think that in that line the rose is red for the first time in English poetry for a hundred years." . . .

Distributed throughout Miss Stein's books and in the *Lectures in America* can be found an account of her successive discoveries and aims as a writer. She did not admit that the word "experiments" be applied to them. "Artists do not experiment. Experiment is what scientists do; they initiate an operation of unknown factors in order to be instructed by its results. An artist puts down what he knows and at every moment it is what he knows at that moment. If he is trying things out to see how they go he is a bad artist." A brief recapitulation of the history of her aims will help us to understand her work.

She left Radcliffe College, with William James's warm endorsement, to study psychology at Johns Hopkins University. There, as a research problem, her professor gave her a study of automatic writing. For this work she called upon her fellow students—the number ran into the hundreds—to serve as experimental subjects. Her interest, however, took an unexpected turn; she became more absorbed in the subjects' varying approach to the experiments than in the experiments themselves. They entered the room with alarm, with docility, with bravado, with gravity, with scorn, or with indifference. This striking variation reawoke within her an interest which had obsessed her even in very early childhood—the conviction that a description could be made of all the types of human character and that these types could be related to two basic types (she called them independent-dependents and dependent-independents). She left the university and, settling in Paris, applied herself to the problem. The result was the novel of one thousand pages, *The Making of Americans,* which is at once an account of a large family from the time of the grandparents' coming to this country from Europe and a description of "everyone who is, or has been, or will be." She then went on to give in *A Long Gay Book* an account of all possible relations of two persons. This book, however, broke down soon after it began. Miss Stein had been invaded by another compelling problem: how, in our time, do you describe anything? In the previous centuries, writers had managed pretty well by assembling a number of adjectives and adjectival clauses side by side; the reader "obeyed" by furnishing images and concepts in his mind and the resultant "thing" in the reader's mind corresponded fairly well with that in the writer's. Miss Stein felt that the process did not work any more. Her painter friends were showing clearly that the corresponding method of "description" had broken down in painting and she was sure that it had broken down in writing.

In the first place, words were no longer precise; they were full of extraneous matter. They were full of "remembering"—and describing a thing in front of us, an "objective thing," is no time for remembering. Even vision (a particularly overcharged word), even sight, had been dulled by remembering. The painters of the preceding generation, the Impressionists, had shown that. Hitherto people had known that, close to, a whitewashed wall had no purple in it; at a distance it may have a great deal of purple, but many painters had not allowed themselves to see purple in a distant whitewashed wall because they remembered that close to it was uniformly white. The Impressionists had shown us the red in green trees; the Postimpressionists showed us that our entire sense of form, our very view of things, was all distorted and distorting and "educated" and adjusted by memory. Miss Stein felt that writing must accomplish a revolution whereby it could report things as they were in themselves before our minds had appropriated them and robbed them of their objectivity "in pure existing." To this end she went about her house describing the objects she found there in the series of short "poems" which make up the volume called *Tender Buttons*.

Here is one of these:

Red Roses

A cool red rose and pink cut pink, a collapse and a
solid hole, a little less hot.

Miss Stein had now entered upon a period of excited
discovery, intense concentration, and enormous produc-
tivity. She went on to writing portraits of her friends
and of places. Two of her lectures in *Lectures in
America* describe her aims in these kinds of work.
She meditated long on the nature of narration and wrote
the novel *Lucy Church Amiably*. This novel is a description of a landscape near Bilignin, her summer home
in the south of France. Its subtitle and epigraph are:
"A Novel of Romantic Beauty and Nature and which
Looks Like an Engraving . . . *'and with a nod she
turned her head toward the falling water. Amiably.'*"

Those who had the opportunity of seeing Miss Stein
in the daily life of her home will never forget an impressive realization of her practice of meditating. She
set aside a certain part of every day for it. In Bilignin
she would sit in her rocking chair facing the valley she
has described so often, holding one or the other of her
dogs on her lap. Following the practice of a lifetime
she would rigorously pursue some subject in thought,
taking it up where she had left it on the previous day.
Her conversation would reveal the current preoccupation: it would be the nature of "money," or "masterpieces," or "superstition," or "the Republican party."
She had always been an omnivorous reader. As a small
girl she had sat for days at a time in a window seat in
the Marine Institute Library in San Francisco, an en-
dowed institution with few visitors, reading all Elizabethan literature, including its prose, reading all Swift,
Burke, and Defoe. Later in her life her reading remained as wide but was strangely nonselective. She read
whatever books came her way. ("I have a great deal of
inertia. I need things from outside to start me off.")

The Church of England at Aix-les-Bains sold its Sunday School library, the accumulation of seventy years, at a few francs for every ten volumes. They included some thirty minor English novels of the 'seventies, the stately lives of colonial governors, the lives of missionaries. She read them all. Any written thing had become sheer phenomenon; for the purposes of her reflections absence of quality was as instructive as quality. Quality was sufficiently supplied by Shakespeare, whose works lay often at her hand. If there was any subject which drew her from her inertia and led her actually to seek out works it was American history and particularly books about the Civil War.

And always with her great relish for human beings she was listening to people. She was listening with genial absorption to the matters in which they were involved. "Everybody's life is full of stories; your life is full of stories; my life is full of stories. They are very occupying, but they are not really interesting. What is interesting is the way everyone tells their stories"; and at the same time she was listening to the tellers' revelation of their "basic nature." "If you listen, really listen, you will hear people repeating themselves. You will hear their pleading nature or their attacking nature or their asserting nature. People who say that I repeat too much do not really listen; they cannot hear that every moment of life is full of repeating. There is only one repeating that is really dead and that is when a thing is taught." She even listened intently to dog nature. The often-ridiculed statement is literally true that it was from listening to her French poodle Basket lapping water that she discovered the distinction between prose and poetry.

It can be easily understood that the questions she was asking concerning personality and the nature of language and concerning "how you tell a thing" would inevitably lead to the formulization of a metaphysics.

191

In fact, I think it can be said that the fundamental occupation of Miss Stein's life was not the work of art but the shaping of a theory of knowledge, a theory of time, and a theory of the passions.